THE REVIVAL OF THE LITURGY

THE REVIVAL OF
THE LITURGY

edited by

FREDERICK R. McMANUS

HERDER AND HERDER

1963
HERDER AND HERDER   NEW YORK
232 Madison Avenue, New York 16, N.Y.

Nihil obstat:

Edward C. Foster
Censor Librorum

Imprimatur:

† Robert F. Joyce
Bishop of Burlington
August 8, 1963

Library of Congress Catalog Card Number 63–18154

To GODFREY DIEKMANN
IN GRATITUDE FOR TWENTY-FIVE
YEARS OF *Worship*

CONTENTS

1

Gift for Father Godfrey Diekmann on His Jubilee as Editor of Worship

H. A. REINHOLD

At first nothing seems easier than my task: to write about a beloved and loyal friend, Godfrey Diekmann, the monk from St. John's Abbey and professor of dogmatic theology at St. John's University, on the occasion of his twenty-fifth anniversary as editor of the monthly, *Worship*. Fortunately, we too now have this custom of collecting articles and essays into a book for a man we want to honor. In the old days Europe had a monopoly in this field with its many *Ehrengaben* and *Mélanges*. But now we are privileged to continue this custom: when we want to honor an academician, we gather his friends, they appoint an editor and he in turn collects short articles, preferably in the field of the *honorandus*. This is more impressive than the purple, which a friend once called "a garment dyed in the juice of sour grapes." Because this tribute lasts and is flattering: Everyone can see how much love, affection, esteem, and work went into it. It is also useful and appropriate, because it advances knowledge, often in a recondite field. What could be more appropriate than to see your friends busy writing for you. This is the truest gift for the academician: to be recognized as a master and to be rewarded with the crown of achievement in a field of common endeavor. I am sure that all will agree with me that Godfrey Diekmann, in all his modesty, deserves this gracious gift. I should know, because I am one of the older contributors to his magazine, and was for fifteen years a monthly contributor. I say this less in vainglory, than to establish myself as among the generation for whom all this is a thing of the past, the dark ages of the Liturgical Movement.

The very size of our country is a reason why something like the Liturgical Movement has had such a hard time in getting a foothold and in bearing fruit. How can a Catholic in Oregon know what has been done in Vermont or Massachusetts? To this we must add the different "national" backgrounds and traditions of the faithful in this country. The Germans and Slavs have a tradition of singing in their churches, while the Celts follow the Mass with silent reverence in order to let the "hedge priest" escape from his pursuers as fast as he can. The Romance-language peoples act differently again, which becomes nowhere as evident as in the "Italian Mission" at Brompton Oratory, where the liturgy is embalmed by the will of the priests who run the church according to Father Faber's infatuation with post-baroque Rome. These differences are easily multiplied and the poverty and far separation of Catholics from each other add yet other reasons for the slower development and thus the uniform growth of the Catholic parish and religious life in this country. In view of these facts, the general remedy for all cases in doubt has been to stay as close to Trent as possible: It was safe and prudent. No sooner had the Catholic put foot on American shore than he took refuge under the umbrella of Trent, and the United States became the most Tridentine country on earth. What was apparently settled by the council of Trent was with great fidelity observed. The great trees in the Church were Trent and Canon Law and the underbrush covering the space between these trees was the growth of the "Old Country" tradition.

Godfrey Diekmann is of German, to come closer, Westphalian stock. His own sense of humor attests that without doubt; it is not Irish anyway. It is true of other apostles of the liturgical renewal in the Midwest. To mention only a few, there are Martin Hellriegel, Reynold Hillenbrand, William Busch. These are only the "post-apostolic fathers"—there are probably a hundred more by now. They differ in one aspect from what we might call the New England school, or more closely circumscribed, the Boston group: Fathers Shawn Sheehan, McManus, Leonard, and a score more in the different seminaries and places of learning.

If one could differentiate these two groups, one might say with a certain justification that the Boston group is the learned one, and that the Midwest represents applied learning. Boston's background is Irish. The immense territory of the Far West, the Southwest, and the South, have partially followed these two dominant groups. In any case these two great liturgical regions are hardly topped now.

The names of Bishops Buswell, Reed and many a still silent worker hold great promise for the future, for they are hardly bound by Old Country nostalgia, they object less to genuine change than the more hidebound East and the more advanced Midwest. The latter suffers from repristination of the "good old days" in Europe, while the East resents anyone who touches even the most encrusted, and in itself hardly meaningful, usage.

On this turbulent sea appeared the good ship *Worship*, or as it was then a bit incongruously entitled, *Orate Fratres*. Like all things done by Virgil Michel, it was a daring piece and he was not afraid of the billows of adversity. He died much too early, if I may be permitted a correction of Providence, and left the monthly to Godfrey Diekmann, who with great *pietas* conserved its outward form. Father Godfrey steered the vessel through plenty or scarcity unafraid, and with a conscience filled with trust and optimism.

Apart from his knowledge and experience, Godfrey Diekmann has in twenty-five years given shelter to the ideas of many an author of bold vision: the evening Mass, the use of modern languages in the liturgy, the restored diaconate, the coming theology of the layman, the thorough reform of the liturgy, the ecumenical movement, the social demands on the Christian of our day, the new kerygmatic attitude in teaching and Scripture, all of these and many more found their expression first of all, or at least in the beginning of their struggle, in the magazine edited by Godfrey Diekmann, with his kind approval, and with a word of commendation.

In reality this relatively small and not too much read monthly contributed a great deal to changing the face of the American Church, and often was the only link with Europe, especially during the war years. Many a European Catholic, who had weird notions about American Catholicism as an externalized, obedient, and spineless brand of the Universal Church, woke up to another reality when he saw

Worship and in it the report on life and applied faith on these shores.

Not that Godfrey Diekmann's influence was limited to his magazine and its few thousand readers; it evoked parallel movements, like a mystical awakening: it influenced the social apostolate, it gave Christian art a steadier course, and housed for several years the biblical renewal, which it kept under its shelter in the days when its survival was seriously threatened. This is what a single man with devoted collaborators is able to do and to do well, when he is unafraid, convinced, and has that amount of charity with which Godfrey Diekmann is so richly endowed.

Father Godfrey used to make me angry, when he disclaimed having a talent or two as an English writer. And this at a time when he used to correct my own contributions. I know that he not only corrected them, he improved them, and retyped them, and thus I acknowledge gladly and publicly a private debt.

If I am not misinformed, it is the task of *Worship* to inform its readers of the latest developments here and abroad, at the center of the Church and at the periphery, to explain the liturgy, to point to those explanations which are above the average, and to provide prudent leadership for its readers. Who will doubt that Godfrey Diekmann has done this with a rare degree of perfection and often under adverse circumstances? And who will wonder that his fame as a theologian, retreat-master, and spiritual director has crossed the borders of our nation? Bubbling with enthusiasm, with an optimism that sometimes seemed to be sheer madness, he has a calmness when flattered that shows his self-control.

The great thing is not that the magazine, Worship, did not founder but kept afloat so many years, although that is achievement in itself, but that it is lively and interesting. The Abbot of Glenstal in Ireland told me, unsolicitedly, that he would not have stayed sane during the war years' isolation, had it not been for Worship. It was his monthly breathing period during that breathless time.

The greatest thing is the power of rejuvenation Father Godfrey has always shown: instead of HAR there is now the beloved Monsignor Casey whose style can set a doorknob acrying or rather laughing. Father McManus has shaped the country according to a more intelligent interpretation of liturgical law. Mother Sullivan makes a good show of her widely-read and intelligent familiarity with the men and women outside the pale. Father Clifford Howell can make the driest subject weep and laugh. He needs no introduction. Nor do I have to give a complete list of all the collaborators. We know them and so does Dom Godfrey. Worship was kept together by wondrous forces and so were we the readers. Where would we have gone for such courageous and yet so orthodox information?

There is only one wish: may he stay with us many years yet in ineluctable courage and bold vision.

2

SCRIPTURAL-LITURGICAL DEPTH
IN CHRISTIAN LIVING

CARROLL STUHLMUELLER, C.P.

At no moment does the Church live so intensely and proclaim so effectively her life in Christ Jesus as she does during liturgical worship. Those who come together for prayer,
St. Paul wrote, "*proclaim* the death of the Lord until he
comes" (1 Cor 11:26). The apostle here employs the same
Greek word *kataggello*, which he used earlier for apostolic
preaching (1 Cor 9:14). Worship is the most eloquent
form of preaching, for it absorbs the Christian in the mysteries of his faith, and in union with his fellow believers he
witnesses to the world the Passion-Resurrection of Jesus.

St. Paul's statement, however, is important, not only for
the key word "preaching," or "proclaiming the death of the
Lord," but also for the other expression: "until he comes."
That last phrase reveals the compelling power of the liturgy
to teach and apply the mystery of Christ in a most practical
way. Worship alerts the Christian to the coming of the
glorified, risen Lord in each event of the day. Christians are
men thoroughly God-conscious, awaiting Him "until he

comes." For this reason they greet one another with *Marana tha! Come, Lord!* (1 Cor 16:22; Ap 22:20).

St. Paul, it seems, is attributing to the liturgy the power to form intelligent, apostolic Christians. This essay concentrates upon the educational force of the liturgy, its ability to give directions for intelligent Scripture study and to impart attitudes for enthusiastic Christian living. In the early part of the essay we move from our present liturgical worship back to the ancient Bible. We will then be in a position to consider the Scriptures as liturgical documents of Old and New Testament times. From this biblical-liturgical depth, we will proceed to the second and major part of this essay. Here we will reverse the process and move forward from the ancient biblical worship to our present liturgy and beyond the limits of the Church ceremony to the fullness of Christian living.

At the very beginning one can raise the question: Why is the present Christian liturgy so important for Bible study? Why is the liturgy more effective than any other means of instruction, "more efficacious than even the most weighty documents of ecclesiastical teaching?" By asking the question in that way, it is already answered. Those words have the authority of Pope Pius XI and come from his encyclical *Quas primas,* on Christ the King.

The Holy Spirit put those directives of Pius XI into action by having the schema on the liturgy placed first before every other item on the agenda of the Second Vatican Council. With God the switch to the liturgy was no last-minute decision; with great care He was making sure that the liturgy provided the context for considering everything else about the Church, Scripture included. The Christian must approach doctrine and life in the Bible in the same way as the Church in solemn assembly—through the liturgy.

There is another strong argument why the liturgy is important for Bible study. It is found in the traditional formula, almost as sacred as any word of Scripture: *Legem credendi lex statuat supplicandi,* "Let the rule for prayer determine the rule for belief." Explained in one way, certainly valid and acceptable, that statement invites us to investigate *how* the Church *prays* if we would know *what* the Church *believes.* Another, and I think truer way of measuring the full import of that classic formula is to remember: when we pray with the Church, we are personally absorbed into the most intense moment of Church life, and from the experience of that moment we can repeat St. John's attestation: "To you we proclaim what *we have seen and heard*" (1 Jn 1:3).

According to St. John, a Christian is not so much a scholar as he is a *witness* proclaiming what he himself has experienced: that the Lord Jesus lives. In the liturgy the Christian beholds the *parousia* or *epiphaneia* of the gloriously risen Christ. Dogma comes to life and the Christian cannot but speak with boldness of what he has seen and heard (cf., Acts 4:13, 20). Religion without liturgy is the Passion without the Resurrection, a dead body laid out to be examined, rather than a living person to be worshiped. Without the liturgy Christians stand condemned by the desperate words of St. Paul: "If Christ was not raised [from the dead], then our gospel [proclamation, *kerygma*] is null and void, and so is your faith" (1 Cor 15:14).

For still another reason, liturgical worship and scripture investigation must maintain very close ties, so that each

draws its truest and fullest meaning from the other. By studying sacred doctrine in the context of liturgical worship, the
Christian anticipates the direction and the contribution of
modern biblical scholarship. He enters the *Sitz im Leben*,
or life-situation, of biblical passages.

That is a broad statement and it needs qualification. It
could be taken disastrously to mean that prayer dispenses
with scholarship. We might rephrase the statement in this
way: if in the past, Scripture had been taught and read with
a keen sense of its constant liturgical use in Israel and in the
apostolic Church, then the discoveries of the contemporary
scriptural movement would not have taken the Catholic
theologian, religion teacher, or Bible reader by surprise. He
would have realized all along that the Scriptures emerged
from the people of God at prayer rather than from the
scholar at study. He would have been aware that very many,
if not most, biblical passages present, not an eye-witness
record of the past, but, instead, a liturgical acclamation of
praise, a credal confession of faith, or a humble prayer for
forgiveness. The Bible would thus have been interpreted as
a proclamation of the redemptive acts of God, not so much
as these were experienced for the first time, but as they were
relived continuously by later generations in Israel or in
apostolic Christianity. Right here we are at the heart of
form-criticism, one of the conspicuous elements of serious
biblical study.

For our purpose right now, we can conclude that only a
small part of this reliving of God's acts of salvation resulted
from study and that one of the most important contributions came from prayer. For depth of understanding, then,
we must approach God's word in the liturgical spirit with
which it was composed.

Let us now examine briefly *how* liturgy can become an important factor in the understanding of Scripture. We will proceed from biblical liturgy to greater depth in two closely related and almost overlapping areas: Christian liturgy and Christian living. "Christian liturgy" confines itself to acts of worship in church; "Christian living," to attitudes and actions outside of church.

If one of the correct approaches to the Bible is through liturgical prayer, then we must begin our study of the Old Testament against the background of Israel's worship and our investigation of the New Testament against the setting of the apostolic liturgy.

In ancient times the sacred traditions were transmitted in a way quite different from our manner of handling the Bible. During most of the Old Testament period and the apostolic times, there was a continuous process of adaptation and modification of biblical traditions and writings. For us today, the Bible is a sacred book, fixed and unchangeable. Out of reverence we would never dare add a new word, much less a new sentence to the Scriptures; our reflections and applications are confined to introductions, footnotes, and commentaries. It was not so in biblical days. The Israelite priests and prophets introduced their reflections into the very fabric of the sacred account.

Songs and confessions of later ages were inserted into earlier traditions. The blessings of Jacob (Gn 49) and of Moses (Dt 33) probably originated in a sanctuary service with the levitical priests begging God to fulfill the hopes of the early patriarch and the lawgiver. Prophecies of Michea and Jeremia, once directed against the northern kingdom of Israel, were later redirected against the southern kingdom of Juda. In the postexilic age, a hymn of thanksgiving was appended to the famous book of Emmanuel (Is 7–12). A careful study of the style and purpose of these various changes points to the *sanctuary* as the spot where this growth took place.

Priests and levites were the responsible agents, and their intention was most clearly revealed in a passage of Deuteronomy. Long after the Mosaic age, a levite repeated these words to the people gathered for sanctuary worship:

> Hear, O Israel, the statutes and decrees which I proclaim in your hearing *this* day, that you may learn them and take care to observe them. The Lord, our God, made a covenant *with us* at Horeb [i.e., Sinai]; not with our fathers did he make this covenant, but *with us, all of us* who are *alive here this day.* He spoke with you face to face on the mountain . . . (Dt 5:1–4).

The levitical preacher did not want the words of Israel's lawgiver simply admired as library curiosities. They were to be experienced as vital forces. In this actualization of the ancient Mosaic heritage, later generations were being called out of a "spiritual" Egypt of sin, to wander through a "spiritual" Sinai desert of sorrow where they meet God "face to face," and in that meeting arrive at the "spiritual" promised land of divine peace. What our scripture textbooks call "typology" was constantly at work in biblical days. We, for our part, add a footnote to the page of Exodus, informing the reader that Moses, the exodus or the covenant are types of conversion to Christ, eucharistic "Bread in the wilderness," or journey to heaven. The Deuteronomist put *his* footnote right into the sacred text. As is quite clear from the style of Deuteronomy, the occasion of *Sitz im Leben* was liturgical worship.

Psalm 94 is an invitational hymn, sung during a liturgical

procession in the temple courtyard. The assembly praised God for creating and redeeming Israel. When the procession arrived at the sanctuary, a priest then delivered this solemn oracle or warning:

> Oh, that today you would hear his [God's] voice:
> "Harden not your hearts as at Meriba. . . .
> Forty years I loathed that generation. . . .
> Therefore I swore in my anger:
> 'They shall not enter into my rest' " (Ps 94:7–11).

Even though the congregation was already living in the Promised Land and was actually worshiping at one of its sanctuaries, still, today they were spiritually back in the desert, hardening their hearts as the Israelites did against Moses at Meriba. Centuries after the psalmist lived, the epistle to the Hebrews quoted this same text, and, in the spirit of the Old Testament poet, actualized it for the Christian worshiper:

> Exhort one another every day, while it is still today, that none of us be hardened by the deceitfulness of sin. For we have been made partakers of Christ. . . . There [still] remains, therefore, a Sabbath rest for [us,] the people of God (Heb 3:13; 4:10).

This rereading or actualization was made possible for the apostles and their first disciples through the gift of the Spirit on Pentecost. Jesus had already announced that the apostles would find a new insight into the Old Testament Scriptures and even into His own words.

> The Holy Spirit . . . will bring to your minds whatever I have said to you. When he, the Spirit of truth, has come, he will teach you all the truth. . . . He will glorify me, because he will receive of what is mine and declare it to you (Jn 14:26; 16:13 f.).

The apostles would never have contented themselves with what they had seen, heard, and understood before Pentecost. After the descent of the Holy Spirit, they proclaimed with boldness—a favorite word of the Book of Acts—the glory or wondrous presence of the risen Saviour. The events and words of Jesus of Nazareth were transfigured, as was Jesus Himself, and became *living* realities, known precisely because they were relived in the apostolic Church. Even sorrow endured by the apostles became a *thlipsis* for the revelation of the messianic Christ (2 Th 1:4–10), so that, in the words of St. Paul, the Christians were "always bearing about in our body the dying of Jesus, so that the life of Jesus may be made manifest in our body" (2 Cor 4:10).

The Eucharist provides an excellent example of how the liturgy absorbed the suffering of the apostolic Church and thereby provided new insight into the breaking of bread. Comparing the eucharist account in Acts and in First Corinthians, we cannot help noticing, as did Hans Lietzmann long ago, the important differences of mood and attitude. The Book of Acts puts the breaking-of-the-bread ceremony in a setting of "gladness and simplicity of heart" (Acts 2:46). St. Paul, on the contrary, stresses the sacrificial motif and states explicitly that the Eucharist "proclaims the death of the Lord" (1 Cor 11:26). Sacrifice was always present in the eucharistic service since its institution by Jesus at the sacrificial meal of the Last Supper. But the Mystical Body of Christ had first to suffer, before she would fully understand the sacrificial meaning of her eucharistic body. Between Acts and First Corinthians stand the persecutions of the Pauline churches.

With this background of history and liturgy, a person is prepared to make the application to his own age. He is reminded that he will never know the meaning of the sacrifice of the Mass until he willingly and obediently suffers for his life in Christ. It is at liturgical prayer, more than at any other moment, that the Christian feels his thoughts fuse with those of Christ and his own sorrows reveal the meaning of the sacred Passion.

In much the same way, the liturgy presents the other mysteries of the life of Jesus. The liturgy is like another Pentecost, transfiguring before our eyes the words, the deeds, and, above all, the person of Jesus. This fact will explain, I believe, the arrangement of the liturgical year which does not place the account of Jesus' ministry and teaching in the period after Epiphany but in the weeks after Pentecost. If the liturgy followed the chronology and the geography of Christ's life, these events would be spread between Christmas and Holy Week. What we find, instead, is the reliving of Our Lord's life in the Sundays after Pentecost. In the power of the Spirit, the life of Christ is our life today, and as we live that life in liturgical worship, we come to "know Christ and the power of his resurrection and the fellowship of his sufferings" (Phil 3:10).

If this biblical-liturgical depth of union with Christ had been the framework of the religion program in our schools, we never would have become obsessed with names, dates, and places in a course entitled "Life of Christ." The "Life of Christ" would have remained what it is in the Bible and in the liturgy, life in Christ through liturgical renewal.

Advent would proclaim the "birth" within us of a new, more vigorous life. This life can only be that of the risen Christ; no other Jesus exists! The triumphant Lord comes, destroying sin in what the Bible and the liturgy call a burst of glory. Christ comes wondrously fulfilling all promises, majestically judging the world in justice. "Glory" is here understood in the biblical meaning of the theophany of God in a great redemptive undertaking; "justice" likewise means that God is "just" in living up to His goodness and in accomplishing His promises. "Judgment," as in 2 Thessalonians 1:3 ff, announces the eternal defeat of the powers of darkness and the establishment of the glorious kingdom of God. These biblical themes dominate the liturgy of Advent, where the Gospel for the first Sunday sounds the trumpet of the final day and the Office repeats the Isaian refrain, "Let justice descend, O Heavens, like dew from above. . . . Let the earth open and salvation bud forth" (Is 45:8).

If time permitted, this treatment of life *in* Christ could be expanded by referring to the literary forms of the Gospels or by studying the varying motifs within each separate Gospel. We must even pass over another important area of investigation: the biblical-liturgical concepts of blood, sacrifice, and redemption. That study would impart a new and different dimension to our knowledge of the Mass. It would take our interest off such notions as death and destruction, substitution and ransom, and stress, instead, the more genuinely biblical concepts of life, union, and the redemptive acts of God. It is necessary that we move on to another practical aspect of how biblical liturgy imparts greater depth, this time not so much to the Christian liturgy but rather to Christian *living*.

The Scripture, the liturgy, and the daily life of the People of God interrelate very closely and develop with constant dependence upon one another. What happens in one area immediately reacts upon the other. What was true in biblical days must still be true today in the continuance of salvation-history. We want to determine, therefore, some of the effects of biblical-liturgical studies upon contemporary Christian living. Nowhere, it seems, has the impact been more noticeable than in the ecumenical movement. Rather than limit ourselves to Catholic-Protestant relations, we want to follow the trend toward unity according to a plan outlined by good Pope John. As a first goal, the pope was seeking to establish a strong, vibrant spirit within Catholicism. Only after that is the Church ready to open her doors to attract her separated brethren.

When Catholics assemble for the liturgical proclamation of Scripture, the Bible is more than a lesson book to be studied, just as the liturgy is more than a ritual to be enacted. Each one must pray, and that means to relive the mysteries of salvation at that deep point of personal existence where each one is himself, distinct from everyone else. While the liturgy maintains the strong, personal aspect of all genuine prayer, it never succumbs to any narrow subjectivism. In the liturgy, each one perforce participates in the prayer of every one.

There is a complaint voiced very often against the liturgical prayer of the Psalms. A person grumbles: "These prayers are not mine, because they do not express my thoughts and my reactions." This is a serious charge against the liturgy, for the Psalms constitute the bulk of liturgical prayer. The complaint goes something like this: "I am feeling happy and joyful, and yet when I open my Missal for the Mass prayers, I must say to God: 'Put an end to my afflictions and my sufferings, and take away all my sins.' [Ps 24:18] On another day, I have a headache, the school team has just lost the basketball game, and there are exams just ahead. The liturgy

tells me to pray: 'Shout joyfully, all you on earth, my praise
to the glory of his name' " (Ps 65:1 f).

This species of complaint against the liturgy, like grum-
bling about exams, proves that the Psalms, like exams, are
necessary. The Psalms pull a person out of his psychological
introversion and thrust him into the Church at large. Americans need to be reminded that there are Cubans and Hun-
garians at the edge of despair; healthy people must remember that there are brethren lonely, hungry, and dying. At the
same time, no persecution can be so black and no famine so
oppressive as to remove joy and peace. In fact, in the very
moment of sorrow, obediently and lovingly endured, there
is a victory like that of the dying Jesus—a victory which
possesses within itself the power of the Resurrection. The
liturgy brings all men together, so that what one person
lacks the other person supplies, "for the building up of the
body of Christ, until we all attain to the unity of the faith
and of the deep knowledge of the Son of God" (Eph.
4:13).

The liturgy thus keeps the worshiper alive to everyone
else in the Church, even to the point of having free men
voice the suppressed anguish of the persecuted, and of having prisoners sing the praise of the joyful. With this background, the CSMC, the Peace Corps, the lay Catholic action
groups, the auxiliaries in hospitals and orphanages are not
activities to absorb spare time; they are necessary expressions of ordinary Christian life.

In the liturgy, more than at any other moment, all are
united in one prayer and one life; divisions break down and
walls collapse (cf. Eph 2:14). A student looking forward to
marriage will not study about the priesthood or religious

life as though he or she were learning about life on the moon! Nor will a boy or girl with a clerical or religious vocation simply tolerate the treatment of marriage as something beneath them. If these subjects are presented with stress upon the ancient and modern liturgical service for the priesthood, religious vows, and marriage, then each will be seen to share one spirit in Christ. Very fruitful would be a Bible Vigil, drawing its texts from Numbers 8 and Exodus 19 wherein the priestly tribe is closely united to the other tribes of Israel; or from those New Testament passages in which laymen in the early Church contribute to St. Paul's priestly knowledge of the mystery of Christ (cf. e.g., Phil 1:3–11, 19, 29 f).

In all these cases, the liturgy is not so much imparting knowledge as it is forming attitudes. Knowledge easily evaporates; attitudes stay for life.

This close interdependence between liturgy and life shows up in a familiar eucharistic text of St. Paul. He wrote to the Corinthians: "he who eats and drinks without distinguishing the body, eats and drinks judgment to himself" (1 Cor 11:29). "Not distinguishing the body" does not imply that the Corinthians rejected the Real Presence. In a *theoretical* way they distinguished or recognized the body of the Lord in the bread which they ate. But in a *real* way they denied it by bickering and jealousy. They had so mangled the body of Christ—His Mystical Body, the Church at Corinth—that the Corinthians no longer recognized the only Christ who exists, the risen Christ who is one with all His members. In the Eucharist they received what they called Christ, but they no longer recognized or distinguished the true Christ. In some way, the Corinthians were unbelievers, trafficking with something most sacred. In this one example it is clear that Scripture demands liturgy, and liturgy demands full Christian life, before a Christian comes to a clear grasp of his faith.

The liturgy, and especially the ancient biblical liturgy, not only imparts a depth of Christian unity among Catholics, but it also extends that spirit of unity to separated brethren. There is no space to develop this point; we must be satisfied with a few instances where the Bible displays a true ecumenical spirit.

Nowhere, it seems at first sight, are Catholics more separated from their Jewish and Protestant brethren than in liturgical worship. We Catholics tolerate and at times even enforce moral and political decisions which we condemn on principle, like divorce and remarriage. A Catholic judge will remarry two divorced persons, so far as the legal aspects are concerned. In matters of dogma, we get together with Protestants for discussion and enlightenment. In liturgical worship, however, the twain meet never, and we each go to the church of our own faith! A Catholic, of course, must worship in a Catholic church, and we do not quibble with that point of canon law, but must we reject everything about Protestant and Jewish liturgy? Must Catholics be totally ignorant about non-Catholic services?

In the Bible we learn that Solomon commissioned Canaanite architects to construct the temple, and they drew its general pattern of courtyard, tabernacle and Holy of Holies according to Canaanite style. Even such details as the Cherubim and the horns of the altar were a customary part of non-Israelite ritual. The texts of religious songs and the melodies for singing them were copied—you might say, plundered—from the Philistines and especially from the Canaanites. Even the agricultural feastdays of local inhabitants were absorbed into the Israelite religious calendar. The spirit of God, we readily admit, was directing these decisions.

The "ecumenical" spirit of the Scriptures may seem to be cancelled out by other biblical phenomena. Before our eyes come those texts of Deuteronomy, authorizing the ḥerem wars against the Canaanites in which everyone and everything of non-Israelite taint were fanatically annihilated. We also recall the Deuteronomic reform of King Josia which leveled to the ground all sanctuaries outside of Jerusalem and strenuously swept the Israelite liturgy clean of outside contamination. Church life in those days, it must be admitted, like Church life today, was not a simple matter of everyone nodding in agreement. There were then, as there are now, strong opinions on both sides.

In the main, the biblical tradition followed a middle path of sanity, and in the whole process of accepting prayer and ritual from outsiders, the Israelites carefully maintained their own religious heritage. Whatever was accepted, was absorbed into their own distinct religious life. Never did it destroy the proper identity of biblical religion. This fact can be exemplified in the case of Canaanite agricultural feasts which the Israelites adopted.

Here we meet the final way, for present consideration, in which biblical liturgy imparts depth to Christian living today. The Bible not only united the believer with his co-religionist and separated brethren. It also kept him right at home in the cosmos or material world where God had placed him to work out his eternal glory.

A union of Israelite and Canaanite religion may seem as incompatible as vinegar and ice cream. Egyptian, Canaanite and Mesopotamian religions were thoroughly *naturalistic*; biblical religion centered just as thoroughly on the great *historical* acts of God. The non-Israelite, religious calendar followed the cycle of nature: dry season and rainy season; virginity, procreation and old age/death. Reacting strongly against these naturalistic cults, Mosaic religion moved around the cycle of God's great redemptive acts in history, like the exodus out of Egypt and the covenant. The Israelites, as already noted, continuously relived these mysteries of salvation.

It gradually became apparent to the Israelites, however, that God fulfilled His promises and renewed the great redemptive acts of history by blessing them with the gifts of nature: with sun, rain, land and crops; with husband, wife, and children. As a result, when the feast of the Pasch commemorated the exodus out of Egypt, the worshipers also thanked God for the creation of the world and for the gift of the barley harvest. In bringing the Israelites out of Egypt, God made them, as He Himself had confessed, "my special possession, dearer to me than all other people" (Ex 19:5). God, of course, would always live up to His obligations which He had then undertaken of fathering and protecting His People. The barley harvest was considered a partial fulfillment of these divine commitments and its festival was joined to the feast of the Pasch.

Pentecost, which liturgically renewed the giving of the law on Mt. Sinai, looked upon the wheat harvest as a blessing of the law upon obedient Israel. The feast of Tabernacles originally celebrated God's care of His People in the desert and the conquest of the land; later it included the final harvest festival of the month of Tishri (September/ October).

This aspect of biblical religion, attributing the gifts of nature to God's extraordinary, redemptive acts, suffused a new glory over the universe. Creation was not viewed as an exhibition of divine power but as a means of renewing the great acts of salvation. To leave a *spiritual* Egypt of sin and to enter a *spiritual* promised land of joy—such was the meaning of the Pasch. Through its celebration, therefore, the Israelites were experiencing the creation of a new heaven and a new earth. The liturgy possessed a "grace" by which this new cosmos was *already* in the process of being established. Each present joy was a taste of the final, messianic joy.

The liturgy, consequently, urged the Israelites, as Pope Pius XII counseled Christians in his 1953 Christmas address, to fulfill the divine command of controlling, using, and enjoying all the material gifts of the world. Scientific progress is an act of obedience to this divine command and partly manifests the glory of the Risen Christ.

The redemption theology, or, we might say, the Passion-Resurrection theology, of the New Testament continues this biblical tradition into our own day. According to the Bible, God will not destroy the universe but transform it. When man is completely tranformed and redeemed, then, as St. Paul wrote in Romans, the earth will no longer groan in travail. The same power of love and obedience which raised Jesus from the dead will infuse new life into all who belong to Christ. This power is at work even now. Miracles which wondrously renew the weakness of nature and consecrate it totally to God's service and man's joy are one part of this resurrection theology; another part is the role of Catholic hospitals and social service; still another part is the vocation of parents, giving and sustaining life in the home.

Nowhere, however, is this eschatological moment more continuously and fully achieved than in the liturgy where everything material is lifted to new grandeur for God's glory and man's joy.

When, then, we ask in conclusion, is the person possessed of biblical depth? He is the one who sinks the roots of his mind deep into the great, redemptive acts of the past, not to live in the past but to relive the *spirit* of the past in the present moment. If a person looks continually to the liturgy, then he will understand doctrine, not as a life of Israel or a life of Christ, but as life *in* Israel and life *in* Christ. The great redemptive moments of the Bible are relived, and in this actualization of the past, God's promises of joy and glory are gradually fulfilled. In their fulfillment, the Christian is tasting even now the great joys of the eschatological age.

The liturgy spans the ages and includes every human reaction; it draws prayers and proclamations from the fullest human experience. Liturgical background, therefore, gives a depth of oneness with Christ's brethren everywhere. Only by being one with all in Christ can a Christian truly distinguish the body of Christ.

Not only does the liturgy integrate each Catholic with all Catholics and even with all his separated brethren, but it also makes him feel right at home on this earth. His roots are deep in every square foot of reality. By his own life in Christ, he is able to transform the universe into the new heaven and the new earth, the new creation of the Risen Christ.

3

THE CONVERGENCE OF LITURGY AND THEOLOGY

MAUR BURBACH, O.S.B.

A proper perspective on liturgy and theology today requires recognition of the fact that theology has suffered from fragmentation for several centuries, so much so that we hardly know any more what it is or what it is about. We speak, sometimes a little too easily, of dogmatic theology, moral theology, spiritual theology, mystical theology, pastoral theology, biblical theology, liturgical theology, and patristic theology as though these were distinct areas, and were universally understood.

The word "liturgical" has fared no better. Here we encounter liturgical theology, liturgical movement, liturgical apostolate, liturgical revival, liturgical art, liturgical vestments, liturgical altars, and liturgical colors.

Such listings of terms, evidence of an unfortunate fragmentation, could be lengthened without effort and almost without limit.

The present direction of liturgy and theology offers a sharp contrast to the diffusiveness now several centuries old.

Today in America liturgy and theology are moving toward the pursuit of wholeness. Attention centers on the Eucharist as source of unification and the means of growth therein.

Theology is knowledge. Liturgy is action. Theology is the knowledge of God, revealed knowledge, the highest knowledge, the science of God and the saints. Liturgy is action, the highest action, the worship of God by the saints in union with the God-man. Theology needs to be worshipful and liturgy needs to be theological. We need to know the God we worship; and we need to worship the God we know.

This reconciliation of mind and heart, of intellect and will, of contemplation and action, of science and love, of the speculative and the practical, characterizes the present status, or rather direction, of liturgy and theology in our land.

Since St. Pius X, repeated papal directives and commands urging "intelligent participation" have touched the deep center of man's conscious and unconscious drives toward this inner reconciliation. The call to "intelligent participation" is a call to wholeness—in liturgy, in theology, and in man. "Intelligent participation" is theological liturgy, and worshipful theology, enjoyed and expressed by God's people.

Theology and liturgy have only one heart animating them both: the Eucharist. But to speak of the Eucharist as the heart of the liturgy and the heart of theology is impossible unless we consider the Eucharist in the full sense as the Word of Life and the Bread of Life. The Eucharist informs and forms the holy People of God; it instructs and produces the Church, the Body of Christ.

The present status of the liturgical revival and the theological revival in America is perhaps happily responsible for an expanding vision of the mystery of salvation and of the pastoral implications of this vision. Gradually, more clearly, we perceive that the liturgy embodies all the vistas of theology. The mystery of salvation is God's loving self-manifestation to His People as history unfolds, realized in the appearance in flesh of His own Son, continued by the Church in the Eucharist celebrated for the eventual gathering to Himself of all His People. This growing, expanding vision points up the inadequacy of those fragmentized glimpses which have so distorted the unified view of the wholeness of God's loving design.

With St. Pius X's call to "return to the altar," the first rays of a new dawn appeared in the Church. A return to the Eucharist, a return to the heart of truth and life, to the whole Paschal mystery, opened up vistas stretching into the past and the future, visions of presuppositions and consequences.

Gone now are the days when liturgy was identified with rubrics and when the liturgical movement was identified with a penchant for lengthened surplices and fuller antependia. Gone, too, are the days when dogma was identified with the recitation of formulae, moral theology with the solution of cases, and Scripture with a sophisticated commentary on isolated texts.

A total theological view is coming into focus, and is finding ever clearer external expression in the liturgy. In a general and basic sense this view arises from the liturgy. As Pius XI observed in 1925: "The annual celebration of the sacred mysteries is more effective in instilling into people the truths of faith and in bringing to them the joys of the spiritual life than any pronouncements, however important, of the teaching Church. These appeal only to a few learned men but once, and then to the intellect, whereas the Church's feasts, which move and teach everyone, go on every year and forever and influence not only the mind but also the heart and the whole man."

Taking the Eucharist for center, as our starting point, we soon see that it makes no sense unless we do it in memory of the Lord, unless we look back to His life on earth and His death, back to His birth and the fulfillment in Him of the whole of salvation history as revealed in the Old Law, back to the Father and His dealings with His People.

But we also see that we must look to the resurrection and the coming of the Spirit, to the formation of a new People of God, to the building up of the very Body of the Lord unto the fullness of the stature of Christ and the final consummation of our encounter with God in total reunion of glory forever. Theology is one vision, and asceticism, mysticism, law, dogmas, history, and preaching have no meaning except in the context of the entire panorama. Study, meditation, private prayers, penitential exercises, all these clarify the vision that comes essentially from the altar where the living word of God is proclaimed every time the eucharistic Bread is broken. Baptism, Confirmation, Penance, Orders, Marriage, and Anointing, the Divine Office, the sacramentals, all these embrace the Eucharist and illuminate it.

But the liturgy, besides providing the vision, also gives it concrete and experiential expression. The whole of life, intellectual, volitional, sensitive, which flows out of and into the Eucharist in a preparatory way, also flows out of it and back into it consequentially until the whole Christ, resurrected in the flesh, achieves the glory of the beatific vision. The Eucharist brings about an ever more penetrating vision and an ever-increasing life of virtue in the people of God, for the upbuilding of the Body of Christ.

Just as supernatural life, in all its elements and aspects is a continuous tide, in ebb and flow, surrounding the Eucharist on all sides, arising from it and returning to it, so too theology, that is, the vision of God and of salvation history, grows not by diversification of separate areas but by an ever more penetrating comprehension of God and His plan.

The Eucharist is the source and center of theological vision because faith comes from it. The other sacraments, other elements of the liturgy, and the proclamation of the Word which belongs integrally to the Eucharist, also have the Eucharist as their center. The Eucharist is also the center of charity and hope, of all the other virtues, and of the totality of Christian life. Or, again, we may say that the Eucharist is the source and center of divine life, of God's life, of its manifestation to God's People, of their experience of it and participation in it.

To be all of this the Eucharist must be infinitely rich. And it must be seen in all its dimensions.

Nothing is more basic than that God communicates Himself to man through signs, through external, visible, sensible things and through the words of His representatives or prophets. And these, whether words or things, or words and things in combination, are sacraments in the widest sense. Sacraments are sacred signs, signs of holy things, or in the last analysis, manifestations of the divine.

It is clear that Christ Himself is the summation of all

sacramentality, for in Him is found the fullness of the Godhead, bodily. Christ, in His body, in His humanity, is the
totality of divine self-revelation to man. He is the consummation of all of God's dealings with man from the beginning, the realization and concretization of the whole Old
Testament. For the Old Testament is more than the words
of Holy Writ; it is all the things and personalities, all the
events and actions and everything else signified by those
words. These are sacraments, constituting a panoramic dis-
play in symbol of the divine. All this is unified in the
humanity of the Word made flesh.

The process of divine self-revelation, however, did not stop
with the bodily ascension of Christ into heaven. On the
contrary, He did not so ascend into heaven until He had
arranged to leave His flesh and blood with us in the
Eucharist as the central efficacious sign and medium
through which His divine life would be experienced and
communicated until the end of time. In fact, the very
product of this communication would be itself a sacramental thing, namely, the growing extension of His very
body, the Church, commissioned in union with Him to
extend and perfect in herself, in her activity, in her
teaching and governing, an ever fuller manifestation of the
divine until God's purpose has been realized in the parousia
of the whole Christ.

This, it seems to me, is the dawning vision of the liturgical movement in our country and everywhere, a vision
which looks into the depths of the Eucharist, or the liturgy,
and finds there first a sign. This sign signifies and produces
the body of the Lord offered to God in worship and offered
to men as food. By eating this food they become the flesh

and blood of the Lord, and so in Him, and one with Him
by the Spirit, return to the Father from whom they came.

The liturgy consists of a great complex of phenomena,
an infinitely rich mosaic panoply of gestures, movements,
sounds, colors, odors, textures, tastes, times, places, and
persons. These are rich and beautiful in themselves and yet
constitute, as it were, only a shell covering, hiding, rather
than revealing, a content infinitely richer. The entire function of this vast array is to bear witness to the sacred, to
the divine, or more accurately, to provide a theophany, an
experience of God.

Central in this great array of phenomena, and more
specifically to the phenomena of the Mass, is the Body and
Blood of Christ, recognized, seen, and tasted only by faith.

This recognition, however marvellous, is not the end of
faith, as is commonly thought, but a beginning of faith.
Faith does not stop with the presence on our altars of the
flesh and blood of the God-man. While it sees in this flesh
and blood the most precious objects in all of creation, it
knows that this presence is not the final marvel. They are
not static objects of our wonder and adoration. Precious
realities though they be, the Body and Blood of Christ is
there as a productive sign, as a sacrament, a divinely fruitful proof that God and man are reconciled and united in
the flesh and blood of the Son of God. Here is the eucharistic, the sacramental, the liturgical summit: God one with
His People through the infinite power of the Spirit in the
one only Body of Christ which is the one, holy, catholic,
and apostolic Church.

The vision here barely sketched cannot be perceived in
the fragmented forms prevalent during recent centuries and

still widely with us. It makes sense only as a whole. When isolated aspects of this great tapestry demand unwarranted attention by their very isolation, disturbing and even destructive results occur. Yet theology continues to be splintered into an ever-growing number of catchy titles for themes or courses, and the liturgy still suffers multiple adjectival attachments to such items as pontifical booties and plastic statuettes widely sold. In such ways, the vision of God's whole design continues to be obscured, and many of the faithful are thus deprived of the fullness of divine life.

Nevertheless, this vision has taken a promising pastoral direction. The making of God's holy People is after all the entire substance both of theology and of liturgy. While these remain distinct—the one a vision, a knowledge; the other an action, the living of the vision—they cannot be separated. They have the same subject and the same goal —the People of God.

Small wonder that both liturgy and theology have taken a pastoral turn. Candles, processions, scholarly reviews, seminary professors, advent wreaths and archbishops all exist for the same thing, God's people, the laity. Once we realize what things are for we can use them properly, turn them in the right direction. The current pastoral orientation in theology and liturgy is the consequence of clearer vision. This focus on God's people, on the Eucharistic Thing, on the Body of Christ, on the Church, so long in coming, guarantees a new flowering in liturgy and theology. Only one caution might be raised, the reminder that God's people are God's, that everything truly pastorally-oriented is God-oriented.

The Liturgical Movement U.S.A. has come a long way

in the past fifty years. It has adopted a theological perspective; on the other hand, it has made a large contribution to theology.

Admittedly there is a long way to go, and new horizons to explore. But courage and hope abound, fostered by warm papal approval during the past decade. Nothing, it would seem could now prevent the full flowering of the liturgical movement and there is the even warmer encouragement, that it is the Spirit, through the liturgy, who continues to form the Body of Christ unto the fullness of God's whole plan.

A great impetus will come from the Second Vatican Council. When it does, let us hope that we will no longer behave like fractious children who have to be dragged along, but like apostles on fire with the Spirit of God.

4

LITURGY AND CATECHETICS

GERARD S. SLOYAN

Let us begin our consideration of the role of the liturgy in catechetics by examining briefly what the work of catechizing is.

It is primarily a matter of forming young people or adults by bringing God's Word to them. It is the work of fashioning the hearers of that Word in Christ. Better still, catechizing is proclaiming the Word so aptly and so unmistakably that the Holy Spirit, the interior Teacher, will find no resistance when He attempts to fashion hearers in the image of Jesus Christ.

Why is it said, hearers? Because the word "catechize" is derived from the basic method of human communication: a sound that echoes in the ear. Printed symbols may come to supplement spoken ones, but the primitive command of Jesus to His disciples entailed a word (*logos*), an utterance (*rhema*), a proclamation (*kerygma*). There can be no faith without hearing; to learn the truth of God, Christ's word (*rhema*) is required (1 Cor 10:17).

The task of forming hearers in Christ by a life-giving

Word is proper to the whole Church. To be baptized is to share in the task. To be confirmed is to receive the fullness of the Spirit which makes certain that the exercise of the catechist's role will come to something in both catechist and child. If we consider the work of parents with their children and of Christian teachers with other people's children, we may say that *most* in the Church have the vocation to form by way of utterance. They must speak God's Word in the family that is His holy Assembly.

Bishops are the chief catechists in the Church. At need they depute others—clergy, religious, layfolk—to help them in the formal work of catechizing. The work goes on informally, however, through the simplest exercise of parental tasks like teaching prayer, explaining about God, "saying Christ" to children in the least word parents speak to them.

Catechizing has as its chief purpose *initiating* students into Christian life, and helping them *persevere* in it once they have been *converted* to it. All three terms have their importance. The formation of young Christians—and adults, for that matter—is by way of induction into Christian life through sacred rites. The term used of old was "mystagogy": a gradual leading of man into that secret design for his happiness that God has treasured within Himself from the foundation of the world. There is no evidence of any divine plan other than that sinful man should be identified with Jesus Christ in His death and resurrection. How? Through the rites of burial and emergence from the waters of baptism, through anointing with chrism to mark the Spirit's descent, through eating the food of Christians as nourishment for the journey of life.

These initiatory rites are the beginning of an existence

"in Christ" which the man new-born can persevere in faithfully only by way of a gift from God. It is, moreover, a life contrary to all that has gone before (even though lived for only days or weeks in infancy), namely the state of inherited guilt or actual alienation from God through personal sin.

The normal progress of the person initiated into Christ, formed in Him, is conversion *followed by communion*: in other words, he turns away from Satan and all that separated him from God and is caught up in a holy fellowship (*communio*) where the good gifts of the redeemed life are all held commonly—the life of grace, the sacraments, all the virtues.

The formation of Christians through progressive initiation into the life of the Church—a life of charity, a sacramental life—will necessarily include some information. The catechist must teach or instruct *while* he initiates and long *after* he initiates. The New Testament is very clear on this. The verb it usually employs to make the point is *didaskein*. The noun for the teaching that is engaged in or conveyed is *didache*. Jesus is the one to whom such teaching is attributed, seldom his disciples; what they must do is proclaim (*keryssein*) the word that the kingdom has come. In our day, however, announcement and exposition, proclamation and teaching must go together. The spread of the Gospel is a fact; all who hear it and wish to live faithfully by it need to have the terms of their new life in Christ explained to them.

Despite the New Testament's emphasis on teaching, the term "religious instruction" does not adequately describe the Church's catechetical task. The chief reason is that

Our Lord in His "missionary command" (Mt 28:19) used the verb *matheteuein* with imperative force. He said "make disciples"; in other words, "make learners who are fully committed to Me and to My cause."

In St. Paul's letter to Philippi, the first chapter, he says that his prayer is that "your *love* may grow ever richer and richer in *knowledge* and *insight* of every kind" (v. 10). Whoever catechizes in the Church does so in a spirit of love (*agape*) for those he teaches. As he teaches he prays that the Spirit will bring not information, "religious truths," to his hearers but *epignosis* and *aisthesis*, the heavenly knowledge and the insight or judgment that help the believer distinguish carefully among persons and things with the very mind of Jesus.

Belief presupposes knowledge, but knowledge is not belief. The devils have faith enough to believe that there is one God and it makes them tremble, says the epistle of James (2:19). "But can you not see, you quibbler [he goes on] that faith divorced from deeds is barren?" So too is religious instruction divorced from divine love and insight and judgment. The danger for all catechists is that their instruction will end in mere knowledge of fact, that their pupils will "know their religion" but not have living faith in God who is a person, and in His Son Jesus.

This is by no means to say that our teaching is to be without content, or without clarity in conveying that content. It must have all these things. But the content of God's Word to us, what He says in addressing us, is something we transmit in all clarity so that a living faith may be aroused. Once this faith has come to birth it must expand and grow in the hearer.

The catechist is committed, therefore, to instruct while forming and form while instructing, not to instruct only, in the catechism class. The pious hope that there will be a carryover elsewhere, whether in the church, in the home, or in everyday life, is foredoomed unless catechists deal with children *whole and entire* when they speak God's Word to them. It is a myth to suppose that the catechism class is simply "the place for learning," that a parental or parochial function is somehow usurped if the child is appealed to in all his faculties or invited by the teaching process itself to have a religious experience.

When God speaks to man it *is* an experience; there is no other word to describe it. We cannot let the word experience be devaluated to connote emotionalism run amuck. Cartesianism has done incalculable harm in Christian catechizing over the years. No specter of evangelistic play on the frayed emotional nerves of children may be raised as the counterargument to this abuse of overconceptualization (which is more generally ververbalization). No one can dispute the truth that the child must be helped to choose the good that is presented to him *when* God speaks. There is no time-payment plan of pedagogy which says, "Learn now, appreciate later." It is only in the world of bad pedagogy that we do that. Adults rationalize in this fashion to explain away their failure to get through to children. The child hears and he sees, he reads and speaks, he moves about and he sings; in a word, he experiences. In ways such as this he comes to know. All these things he does in the one place, the catechism class.

Everyone admits that the primary cause of concern in the modern Church is the divorce of religious knowledge from Christian life. Men do not act in their adult years as they have been taught to do. The secularist spirit is blamed for much of this. Bad parental example is cited. The modern appeal to the passions, to the acquisitive instinct, is bemoaned. All these factors are unquestionably influential. Yet it does not occur to nearly enough catechists that the chief reason for the adult divorce of learning and life is that the two never came to the child together in the first place. At the heart of the adult infidelity is the dissociation of the catechizing process from the reality of Christian life in childhood, whether in the parish church, the family, or the neighborhood. Catechizing is a kind of hothouse bloom related to nothing else in the child's experience: strange words, strange ideas, strange sanctions. Another possibility, all too likely, is that the only thing it is related to *is* the child's Christian life in the parish. Correlation between catechism study and sacramental practice runs very high, both being largely incomprehensible to the child and irrelevant to his life.

The Church cannot Christianize every milieu, it is true. She does have theoretical control, however, over parish churches, over the schools and Confraternity classes run in conjunction with them, over the education of clergy and catechists. She can form the parents of children along with the children themselves. At least theoretically these things are so.

What might we not expect if the catechetical program of the twelve years of school life consisted in a formation in faith rather than "instruction in religion"? Father François Coudreau says that, "All catechesis, because it is the food of faith, should likewise be a launching into supernatural existence, an education toward a personal Christian life. . . . It is an apprenticeship in the life of believing."[1]

What is the present situation in catechetics?

We know that the small child reacts globally, that is to total situations, and that most adolescents and adults as well tend to think in wholes. They react synthetically rather than analytically. Most members of the human race take things in if they are immediate to their experience, concrete. If matters are abstract or require much sorting out, large parts of the population cannot come to terms with them. They are defeated by any such presentation of reality. "I never knew what it meant," they say later on in life, "but I learned it anyway. You had to."

Let us consider the situation of the small child in the ordinary process of learning. He goes to school. It is a situation geared to him. His child nature is catered to in school. He learns there. If the school is conducted by the Church, it may be hoped that he learns what is important about his new life in Christ there. This life is not a thing of the school, however. It is a reality apart from the school as well, indeed largely apart from it. Life in his family, life centered around the neighborhood and the parish church, goes on from day to day. The catechism class tells him what his Christian life means.

"Oh, but you have the whole thing backwards," comes the objection. "You are dealing with this problem out of books. Things go that way in barely one in a thousand cases. To be sure there is a home life, and the parish church exists, and maybe these youngsters have been in it before they start school. More probably they have not. The school or the first communion class is the center of Christian life for most of them. Let's not deceive ourselves with theory. If they don't learn about their religion there, most of them won't get it anywhere."

We said earlier, remember, that the Church cannot

Christianize every milieu but she does have control over some. She is able to control what the schema on liturgy of the First Session of Vatican II calls "the summit . . . and source of Christian life," her own public sacramental worship. What is happening to the child's parents if they are coming to Sunday Mass? Many of them are, uninterruptedly. Many too who have got out of the habit begin to come again when the child does. What is happening to the child when he comes to church? The school or the catechism class needs to be something in relation to this event in church, not the other way around. Formal catechetical training has never been defined as the summit and source of Christian life. It never was and it never will be. In fact, though, it often seems to be that.

We have things woefully in reverse. We have made home life and sacramental life the handmaids of catechism, not the reverse, which is the way things should be. We will never do what is right catechetically until we put the Eucharist at the center and make all else we do revolve about it.

The child in fact does go to Sunday Mass. It is an adult world there, even though pew after pew may be filled with children like himself. It is especially an adult world, because all the children have been put together for safe-keeping.

Some children can interpret this adult world with the help of a child's Mass-book, if they read with pleasure. Certain ones do. Not a great many, but some.

The child may learn awe from silence. Again, some do.

He may learn wisdom from the lips of a priest who can speak to children. Not many priests can. It is worth your life to have such a priest in your parish church, and he always gets transferred. The first day people hear a good children's sermon they come out thinking: "We won't have him long. Surely we can't keep this one long. Or else he'll stay but won't keep speaking to their hearts for very long."

The most likely thing to happen is that the child will squirm and wish the Mass was over, because so little of it speaks to him. We can try to keep him busy there, keep him out of mischief. There is the familiar policing of youth by grown-ups, the low point of Christian community worship. "Yes, but without it?" "Absolute normalcy. They would then express their boredom freely." Holy Mass is chiefly a behavior problem to children, a place they weren't good at six times.

We can try to keep the child busy at the Mass. We do quite a lot of that. Consider our efforts.

There is in the first place choral song, consisting in bad words, sung to bad music, in bad tempo. It needn't be so, of course. It just usually is. No matter if the finest hymns are used, without a director the tempo will lag. This fact inevitably sees to it that the child—including the nonmusical child—comes to identify sacred song not with joy but with what is so aptly termed in today's world "a drag."

We can ask the child to be more active still at Mass. Normally this means assigning him unison recitation. "Unison" is a wonderful word because it stands for a wonderful thing. It means submitting one's personality, signified by the speech or song one produces, to serving one's fellows in community. Univocity is neither pallid nor dead-level in concept, but in fact we make it so. God knows we need not. Several prefaces of the Roman rite lead into the *Sanctus* by speaking of the praise the Christian community joins in offering to the Father, "together with angels and archangels, thrones and dominations, the whole heavenly host *with a single voice.*" A marvelous conception! What participation in the Mass amounts to among youthful populations generally, however, is the monotonous singsong which adults have long ago concluded is proper to childhood. Most children despise this performance in their hearts. It is testimony to adult laziness with respect to them, and they know it. They are started off like a talking-machine. In the same spirit they cooperatively continue.

There exist, it would seem, adult Catholics in large numbers who will do anything as adults to avoid a return to the painful recitative performances they were subjected to in youth. As soon as they learn that certain partial goals of the liturgical renewal are participation in song and recitation they will have none of it.

The child needs to participate in the Church's sacred offices, like any Christian. Normally he has not mastered spoken language well enough to use this instrument comfortably in the work of praise. He needs to sing. This he can do rather well, if he is helped in it. He needs to sing songs, for his whole experience is that what one sings is songs— not lugubrious wails at half-time. He needs to sing in his own tongue, for music is only part of the expressiveness of song, the other part being words. He must respond in song when he is addressed in that medium; the alternative is rudeness. The last thing in the world he needs to do is to grind out laboriously, in the company of his fellows, what is the priest's business anyway: "Ac-cept, O ho-ly Fath-er, al-migh-ty and e-tern-al God, this spot-less host which I, Thy un-wor-thy serv-ant, of-fer to Thee . . ."

Will it ever end? If the children of the nation could be

polled they would name today as the last day for such performances, and they would be right.

If song is the language that befits the child participant
best, there are many other ways that can help him be at one
with the great act in which he is invited to have a part.
High on the list is his movement, his gesture, his overall
comportment. He is in a sacred place: the church. He is
doing a sacred deed in honor of a holy God. All that he
does there must testify somehow to the numinous quality of
the situation. Taking holy water from the font, genuflect-
ing, tracing Christ's cross on brow and heart come immediately to mind as pieces of worshipful behavior.

There are simpler matters that can be of even greater importance, such as standing as a posture of prayer. The
Catholic child has been so conditioned to "flopping," like
the "aggarywating" Mrs. Jerry Cruncher, that any other
stance during the celebration of the mysteries seems im-
pious to him. Like Pavlov's salivating pup, down he goes
at the tinkle of a bell whether he is three sacristies away
or in the middle aisle. There are many Christians who
simply do not know sustained kneeling as an expression of
awe before mystery. No doubt it has its place in the West.
The older and the better sanctioned practice of Christians,
however, is the upright posture in prayer. No unsubmissive-
ness is betokened, only the readiness of spirit that says:
"Here am I, Lord. Send me." The child needs to learn to
pray standing.

Pastors observe that the last matter they succeed at as
they attempt to introduce programs of participation in
stages is getting the people to rise after the consecration.
It has been so dinned into the faithful that Christ's sacra-

mental presence requires bent knees that they experience an invitation to sacrilege when any other course is proposed to them; that and the breaking of silence. The thoroughgoing choral character of the Eastern liturgies is an affront to the normal Westerner, reduced to muteness as he has been in recent centuries for entirely accidental reasons. Yet the most natural human response to a God who speaks to us in symbols is to rise and speak to Him in song.

We mentioned above the fittingness of tuneful hymns in the worship of children. Perhaps even more fitting (because it breaks things into smaller units for them and permits sustained emotional release for its duration) is the acclamation or "pious shout." The Canon is over. A triple "Amen" is sung in successively higher tones and in crescendo. It may even be harmonized. Or again, the first Scripture reading is over. Simplified versions of the gradual or tract in strong musical phrasing can give the word of God a meaning for the child that Paul's difficult argument probably did not supply him with. Most importantly of all, as the Gospel is about to be proclaimed in the child's hearing he can give immediate assent to all it will say and all it will require of him by his outburst of praise:

Lord!"

to you,

ry   O

"Glo-

At the Mass, the homilist (who will normally be the celebrant) and the lector and commentator—if the two roles are separated—must speak to the child about what is really happening. That is why in light of present liturgical structures the highest degree of comprehension is possible at the low Mass accompanied by a brief commentary. In the sung or solemn Mass Latinity increases in direct proportion to song; the engagement of the worshiper in the sacred action decreases in inverse proportion. This fact accounts for the confusion and at times annoyance of those who say, "First the Church sanctioned the missal and the chant. Now she seems to be consigning both to the scrap heap. What can we look for next?" We can look for more of what we have been experiencing, namely progress in the people's participation in rites which become more meaningful through progressive reform.

We have mentioned the ways in which posture and movement can speak to the child. All are effective in their wordlessness, yet all are rendered more effective when there is added to them a spoken word. The priceless and unique Word is that of Scripture, but God can address His people through the prayers of a rite as well. We have intimated the rich possibilities of a commentator here. He is able to cut through the complexities of sacred rhetoric and lay bare to children the heart of a petition or a chant of adoration. There is more. The whole world of sacred symbolism in vesture and appurtenance stands ready to serve God as a tongue to speak to His people.

We are brought to an important question here. Do symbols really teach, or does the symbolism of the liturgy itself need explanation? It would seem that the latter is the case. How many hours have not gone into expositions that begin, "The priest wears a cincture because . . ." "The reason he holds his hands over the chalice at this point is . . . ," and so on? This is so true that the normal catechist is prone to say of symbols, "They are something you explain."

Actually, symbolism exists precisely to save explaining. There is a sense in which a symbol, if it does not teach of itself, can never be made to. Incense is sweet-smelling; it arises in great, billowy clouds before the Lord. What more can be said of it? The fragrant smoke renders any extended comment on its meaning needless. When we apply the water of another font than that of baptism to our brows, tracing the sign of Christ's cross as we do so, what else can the gesture mean but a renewal of the spirit of our baptism —provided it meant all it should have to us in the first place?

In that last phrase we have put our finger on a matter very important to symbolic signification. There must be an element sufficiently common to the sign and the reality it stands for that the symbolism recommends itself to the viewer almost at sight. The only modification that might be made of that statement is that the very young or the culturally deprived need help in learning what their experience has not yet taught them. In the main, however, all effective symbolism is natural. The conventional symbol is based on nature. Witness the striped barber-pole of blood-letting, the red light of danger, and even the history of alphabets.

Water cleanses. It buoys up, and slakes thirst, and drowns. Oil soothes. Bread sustains life. Candles give light. Or take the ordinary materials used in Christian worship such as linen. Is the altar-linen a tablecloth for the child? It is if it is placed on a real table, and is free of the myriad of lacy curlicues that make taking supper on it the last thing that would occur to him. Linen is something that says cleanliness and care to everyone in our culture, even the very poor. In the same way, the rich fabrics of a chasuble or an antependium have a message of the *special* about them. No one dresses or decorates like this except for a high purpose. If vestments are not striking and handsome, then teaching their meaning is a lost cause. "Once the maniple used to be a kerchief for perspiring celebrants." "The stole was a common neck-piece that became our scarf or tie." The youngsters can not be made to care. And when it comes to the allegorical senses of the vesting prayers (except for that of the cincture, which is surely no allegory), they *should not* be made to care. The symbolisms are far too subtle to merit their attention.

The inescapable fact is, however, that when a celebrant enters the sanctuary in procession richly vested the worshipers—even the youngest—have an immediate experience of beauty. "This man is dressed as if he belongs to another world!" is the immediate reaction. If that world is merely the world of the past or of a thousand musty vesting-cases it is a world well lost. Bad vestments, however richly laden, evoke such associations. Good vestments, on the other hand, make people think of a sanctuary not built with hands which lies beyond the veil of the heavens. The ministers who go vested this way are identified unhesitatingly as God's men—the executors of a covenant with the Lord. The worshiper has an instantaneous experience of splendor —and the work of the vestments is done.

The same thing is true of historical details in liturgical rites that no longer have meaning, such as the priest's gesture of placing his hands over the gifts at the *Hanc Igitur*. No amount of telling what the high priest did of old is of much help here, nor of the early Christian priests' gesture over foodstuffs for the poor placed near the bread and wine. The simple outstretching of two hands thumb to thumb, palms down, slowly and reverently, connotes the invocation of the divine unmistakably. Needless to add, it must be seen by all if it is to speak to all.

There is only one road to the fruitful use of symbols, and that is to let the sign speak for the reality. The signs that do this are fine art work produced by honest craftsmen which are readily accessible to the eye. There must be many objects available to the worshipers *for their use* that convey God's holiness to them. Such are processional crosses, candles, hymn and prayer cards, communion patens, indeed the very pews in which they sit. These objects will speak of the mystery of a redeemed creation if they use wood and metal, ink and paper and plastic honestly. The machine is potentially man's great friend but machine-done art is his great enemy. Many modern churches contain no trace of any other kind. (We here cheerfully include mass-produced European woodcarvings.) It is no wonder that religion is judged by many in their adult years to be unreal at best and a fraud at worst. The media of Christian instruction that spoke to them most powerfully in their youth had nothing to say to them but that, once they came to reflect on the way the message was framed, artistically.

The bodily comportment of celebrants and other ministers similarly conveys sacredness through its serenity. A careful rhythm with respect to spoken sacred material does the same. These actions, these words, are the actions and the words of God, the child deduces. Conversely, the acceleration of so many recited Glorias and Credos will say to him that the whole performance is unimportant since its essence seems to be that it needs to be got over quickly.

All these considerations are in some way pre-liturgical.

They concern the conditions that ensure fitting behavior and the proper dispositions for a human act that is transcendent. It is God's act even before it is man's, being His breaking in on man through the action of His Son. Christ acts through the sacraments, we say, and we say it because it is so. What once happened in history—God's deed to save us—happens again and again in sacramental mystery. If this happening is experienced by the child in the new medium, very little need be said about it. If it is not experienced no amount of saying can make the matter either credible or important to him.

Through the liturgy we are engrafted onto the vine which is Christ and become God's tender planning; we are the Saviour's body, His temple, His bride. Because of this intimacy with Him, bordering on identity, in the Nativity we are born of the Virgin; at the Epiphany we perform the first of His signs that made His disciples believe in Him; now we are transfigured with Him in glory, now we die and rise with Him and make ready to go back to the Father's side. All these things we do in symbol. What we perform in a sacramental way we do just as really as in the way of nature. In any action in the order of grace what is unseen is far more important than what is seen, and it is terribly real. The only proof we have of the reality of the invisible is the visible.

The ultimate actuality in sacrament comes through to us by the sign's power to teach. In this order of things, great celebration means great faith and great holiness. Poor celebration means faith from some other source, so little is the inherent power of sacred sign relied upon. It means holiness on terms other than the Church's terms. It means setting at nought the insights of our Fathers in the faith who, having been given sacred signs by the Master, devised rites and ceremonies to accompany them. Together with the sacraments, these are the media of grace which teach the very gift they transmit.

All catechizing has as its purpose bringing persons to maturity in Christ who are already new-born in Him. Retaining the birth figure—well known to the Fathers—we may alter the time references and let baptism be signified by the act of conception. In such case fetal development would stand for the catechetical formation of childhood— all the time it takes to form a human being. Birth would then be the beginning of independent life outside the protective womb of catechetical formation.

What happens in fact, in terms of the analogy? There are natural abortions and stillbirths by the thousands. These are the Christians who do not practice faith after childhood or practicing it, take no joy in it, because what happened in the womb was not developmental. It was protective and well-intentioned. Nourishment, oxygen, cell growth were all provided somehow but it did not form in the image of humanity, the perfect humanity which is Christ. Not stillbirth but safe birth marked by malformation seems to describe the prevailing phenomenon in this country best.

What is the thalidomide that we have been administering to ourselves all these years? If a single dosage must be named it is the catechism almost totally unrelated to profound sacramental doctrine and to sacramental celebration. This will describe any catechism in widespread popular use. The tenor of instruction has been not indifferent to the liturgy but in active opposition to it, if unconsciously. Even when the liturgy was "stressed" in catechizing—and it has been more or less for thirty years—this opposition remained. Liturgy was always defined or described or analyzed, it was not *done*. Like a kiss, the liturgy can endure just so much analysis. In most cases it was described as something so exclusively done by a priest that the true nature of these acts of Christ and His Church were not apparent to the child. Frequently since the papal decrees of 1951, 1955, and 1958, catechetical treatments have actually suppressed or played down the participation aspects of sacramental celebration. This is either from lack of conviction in the writers about the nature of liturgy, or owing to fear of scandalizing teachers and children at the widespread failure of the clergy to conform to prescribed forms of celebration.

How shall we conclude our brief treatment of the liturgy and catechetics? We have tried to show first the nature of the Church's catechetical commitment, then the ways in which *love* and *knowledge* and *insight* come to the child as he celebrates the mysteries. We did not dwell on the way formal instruction and learning through participation got separated historically, assuming it to be known to most readers and not germane to a solution in any case. The whole burden of our remarks has been that the liturgy is unrivalled as a Christian formative influence, even when it has been seriously rivalled in fact by a catechism that did not comprehend the inner spirit of Christian life.

Certain concluding remarks seem indicated. The first is

that unless parish and school communities begin to celebrate the mysteries liturgically, and in their catechism classes begin to learn by way of "celebration," the growth of schools and CCD programs will represent a setback rather than an advance. More pupils mastering the wrong things better is a situation that former decades were able to endure for sociological reasons; future ones can not abide the anomaly.

Secondly, veneration of St. Cerberus, patron of catechetics ("knowing what is right," "knowing what the Church teaches," "knowing the laws of the Church"), needs to go the way of the cult of St. Philomena, and for the same reason: it is a touching story, but it seems never to have happened. Apart from conscious participation in the work of the Church under the headship of Christ nothing Christian exists, least of all a "doctrine" separated from that worshipful behavior which is the proof of love.

Lastly, unless the clergy receives seminary training that makes abundantly clear the liturgical dimension of all the sacred sciences (as the First Chapter of the II Vatican Council's schema on the liturgy enjoins), the improvement of catechetics in this country has no lively prospect.

Because Father Godfrey Diekmann has spent twenty-five years as editor of *Worship* in the work of clerical education (among other things) it is a pleasure to hail him as the leading catechetical figure of our day. Pastoral liturgist, did someone say? But of course it comes to the same thing.

Note

[1] Gerard S. Sloyan, ed., *Shaping the Christian Message* (New York: Macmillan, 1958), p. 139.

5

The Liturgical Formation of Candidates for the Priesthood

WILLIAM O'SHEA, S.S.

To attempt to discuss the liturgical formation of the candidate for the priesthood amounts to speaking of the very training of the priest itself. No man can be adequately trained for the priesthood, in the modern world especially, without having received a sound liturgical training. It is only because so many of us for so long have lost sight of what the liturgy is and if we may dare say so of what the priesthood really is, that we do not see the truth of this at once.

The man who comes to the seminary comes to be made into a minister of Christ and a dispenser of the mysteries of God. The object of the sacrament of Holy Orders, and so of the training that leads up to that sacrament, is to fit him to be a celebrant of the sacred mysteries, a shepherd of the flock of Christ, a physician of souls, and a herald of the Gospel. To put it briefly, he is to be the instrument of Christ to continue His Work in the world. He is the sacrament of Christ, the sacred sign of Christ's effective presence in the world.

On the threshold of his ordination to the priesthood, the ordinand is admonished to reflect seriously on the meaning of the priestly office; "Dearly beloved sons, who are to be consecrated to the priesthood, endeavor to receive that office worthily and, once received, endeavor to carry it out in a praiseworthy manner." The rather long exhortation that follows, and indeed the whole rite of ordination itself, is a careful statement of the Church's own reflection upon the nature of the priestly office and the demands it makes upon those who undertake it. Turning his eyes upon the whole range of priestly activity, the ordaining bishop using the consecrated formulas of the Church's liturgy defines and describes the priesthood by a series of active verbs. "The priest must offer the Holy Sacrifice, he must bless, he must preside and lead, he must proclaim the Word of God, he must baptize." In other words, he must be a priest, a shepherd, a herald of the Word, a dispenser of the sacred mysteries. For this he is blessed and consecrated and set apart—ordained—to continue in the world the redemptive activity of Christ. Everything else that he does flows from this and is conditioned by it.

All the acts enumerated by the Pontifical here are pastoral acts and, specifically, they are *liturgical* acts. A man is ordained to the priesthood primarily to celebrate the sacred liturgy and to lead people into a more fruitful celebration of the mysteries of our redemption. The life-work of the priest is the *aedificatio corporis Christi*, the building-up of the Body of Christ. But that body is built up, brought to full maturity only through the sacraments, and particularly through the Eucharist. Consequently, the formation or training that he receives in the seminary must be directed toward making him an intelligent and effective celebrant of the sacred liturgy, and that can be done only if he sees first of all what the principal role of the priest is. He must be led into the very mystery of Christ, the Priest, by the consonant and reflective celebration of the sacred liturgy, which is nothing less than the exercise of the Priesthood of Christ.

The liturgy is, therefore, not merely one of the seminary disciplines—it is the chief instrument and the principal means of priestly training and so must pervade and inform the entire seminary program. Before being a study or discipline, it is an action, the action of Christ and of His Church. So it is an action that must act upon us to mold and fashion us according to the pattern of Christ the Priest.

Training for the various professions in the world is given largely by means of theory and practice in the science that this professional man will one day practice; adequate preparation for the priesthood demands much more than that. It can only be acquired by life-giving contact with the mystery of Christ, a personal, daily encounter with Christ Our Lord Himself in His saving acts. Without this, the study of theology and the practice of pastoral techniques will be useless. Now, the place where we encounter the saving acts of Christ: the mystery of the Death, Resurrection and Ascension, is the sacred liturgy. The liturgy is the reenactment *in sacramento* and *in mysterio* of the Paschal Mystery.

When we speak of the liturgy here we mean, of course, the *entire* liturgy, the whole complexus or body of signs, words, actions, readings, prayers, chants, that go to make up the worship of the Church. They are the outward and visible signs of Christ's Priesthood in action in our midst. That Priesthood is active not only in those essential rites that make up the seven sacraments but in every rite and every prayer, every reading, that forms the framework or the setting of these seven sacraments. Taken all together they go to make up the totality of the liturgy. Each in its place must receive the attention and the emphasis that is due to it. The reading of the Word of God is not of the same importance as the words of consecration; but without the reading of the Word of God and meditation upon it, the words of consecration will not have the complete and ultimate effect upon us that they are intended to have.

St. Pius X expressed this truth for all time when he said, "The primary and indispensable source of the true Christian spirit is active participation in the most sacred mysteries and in the public and solemn prayer of the Church." The full implications of this are worked out by Pius XII in the encyclical *Mediator Dei*. Among other things he says: "The Holy Sacrifice of the Mass must be for all Christians the center and spiritual source of Christian piety"; and again, "it is an unquestionable fact that the work of our redemption is continued and that its fruits are imparted to us during the celebration of the liturgy, notably in the august sacrifice of the altar." The last quoted words are hardly more than a paraphrase of the teaching of the Secret Prayer of the Mass of the ninth Sunday after Pentecost: "Grant, Lord, that we may take part in these mysteries in a becoming manner, because as often as the commemoration of this victim is offered the work of our redemption is accomplished."

From this it follows that a priestly formation that is not

principally and primarily liturgical formation is a contradiction in terms. The priestly formation must be a Christian formation. Or to put it in another way, the candidate for the priesthood must be a good *Christian* before he can become a good priest. For all Christians, but especially for the priest, the liturgy is the chief source of sanctification. The liturgy is the sanctifying presence of Christ in person. It is the privileged place where Jesus Christ seeks us out, reaches us and lays hold upon us. He penetrates our life and by the celebration of the liturgical mysteries He makes us participate in His own mysteries of holiness.

But the high point of this life which the liturgy places in us by Baptism and develops in us by the Holy Eucharist and the other liturgical rites, is the sacrifice of Christ—offered once and accepted and now made present in the sacred mysteries, especially in the Blessed Eucharist. This sacrifice we call the Paschal Mystery, for the cross cannot be separated from the Resurrection and the glory it leads to: together the Cross, Resurrection, Ascension constitute the *one* mystery of salvation—the Paschal Mystery. By plunging us into this mystery, by bringing us into vital contact with it, the Mass gives us the power to unite our sacrifice with the sacrifice of Christ. Better still, it enables us to reproduce that sacrifice in us. Thus, the Paschal Mystery becomes in truth the center of Christian living as it is already the center of Christian life and worship. Through the Mass, taken as a whole, we are formed in the dispositions and the attitudes of Christ the High Priest of our confession. In no other way can we truly imitate what we handle. We become imitators first of all *in the very act* of the liturgical celebration, then in the whole conduct of our life.

The object of the liturgical celebration is the salvific act (the Life, Death, Resurrection of Christ) really and objectively re-actualized, re-presented, and lived in such a way that the Redemption of Christ becomes a reality under the veil of sacred rites. These sacred rites make us know that we must model ourselves upon the action of Christ, who comes in contact with us through the liturgy. Hence, the importance and the power of the least chant, the shortest reading, the briefest prayer. They all form an indissoluble whole—the action of Christ and the mind of Christ, His states and His attitudes, are mediated to us through the spoken word which gives form to the sacred rite and interprets it for us. The words and actions of the liturgy are a depository of the authentic Christian spirit. They show us what our thoughts and feelings are to be—what response we must make to the revelation of Himself that God gives us in the sacred texts. For the priest, the liturgy is a school of biblical and doctrinal formation because it puts him into direct and immediate contact with the Sacred Scriptures and the dogma of the Church. Even more so, it is a school of spiritual formation, because it makes him enter into the mystery of Christ and brings him into life-giving contact with models of virtue and holiness. Not only does it enable him to contemplate the mystery of Christ and the mystery of Mary and the saints, it furnishes him with the means to realize these mysteries in his own life, to imitate them and to be transformed by them so that, as M. Olier says in his *Pietas Seminarii*, "each one may confidently say of himself what the Blessed Apostle Paul freely said of himself: 'I live, now not I, but Christ lives in me.' "

The Bible forms the framework of the liturgy and the

liturgical prayers. The texts of Missal, Breviary, and Ritual are so pervaded with the Scriptures that the whole liturgy is only one vast contemplation of the history of salvation. Through the celebration of the liturgy we enter into the history of salvation. The sacred rites carry on in our midst the works of God, the "mighty deeds," the *mirabilia Dei* of both the Old and New Testaments. The same God who acted first in the events of sacred history to create, save, and sanctify His People, to make covenant with them and dwell with them, now acts in the same way and to the same purpose, in the sacred mysteries.

The liturgy teaches us the true meaning of the Word of God contained in the Bible. It gives it to us in its proper context, the context of the sacred rite. It shows us that the Word of God comes to us in and through the Church. We see the continuity of the Old and New Testaments: "In order to celebrate the Paschal Mystery, O God, you instruct us by the pages of the Old and New Testament alike." The Church assembles together first in order to hear the Word of God and then to respond to it.

The liturgy is a school of sacred doctrine because it presents all the mysteries of our faith for our contemplation. It is dogma prayed and reflected upon by the Church. The sacred rites open up for us the meaning of the Incarnation, the Redemption, the Assumption of the Blessed Virgin and all the other mysteries, and show us the bearing that these events have upon our lives. They come to us in the liturgy not as abstract truths but as realities glowing with life *ut dum Deum visibiliter cognoscimus, per hunc in amorem invisibilium rapiamur.* To enter into the world of the liturgy is to drink from the living wells of doctrine pure and undefiled.

The liturgy teaches doctrine in another way in the sense that it is, as Pius XI said, "the ordinary organ of the Church's magisterium." It reflects the teaching of the Church, not partially or one-sidedly, but completely and totally, according to the maxim *Legem credendi stat lex supplicandi.* By the liturgy, doctrine becomes our daily food, nourishing our faith and stimulating our devotion. Strengthening our belief, it opens up to us the treasure-house of sound teaching, and daily enriches us with the treasures that sound teaching contains. For the priest it is the great source of preaching and catechesis—and this is not only because it contains all that he must teach to others, but it shows him the way in which he is to communicate religion to others: in a living, dynamic, life-giving way.

Finally, the liturgy is the first school of spirituality for the priest (and so, for future priests) and that simply because of what the liturgy is: the real, objective re-actualization, re-presentation, and re-living of the salvific act of Christ.

The priest participates in the saving act of Christ by entering into the mysteries of his Life, Death, Resurrection and Ascension. Now these mysteries are accessible to us only through the sacraments. "Whatever was visible in the life of Christ," says St. Leo, "has passed over into the mysteries [of the Church]." There we can lay hold upon them and make them our own. "I find Thee in Thy mysteries," cries St. Ambrose. "And these mysteries," said Pius XII in *Mediator Dei,* "are the highest examples of Christian perfection, the sources of divine grace." Already identified with Christ by his Baptism and his ordination, the priest daily identifies himself more closely with Him in the Sacrifice of the Mass. With Christ he becomes still more both Priest and Victim. This is not the language of sentimental emotionalism but the teaching of the Church: "Recognize what it is that you do when you celebrate the sacred mysteries; imitate what you celebrate in order that celebrating the mysteries of the Lord's Death you may be earnest in mortifying your bodies [members] of all vice and concupiscence."

The liturgy is thus inseparable from the effective consecration of our will and our intelligence. We must live what we celebrate. "Celebrating the mysteries of the Lord's Death you may be earnest in mortifying your bodies from vice and concupiscence." When we have made this consecration, we have responded to the exhortation of St. Paul in the Epistle to the Romans: "I exhort you then, brethren, by the mercy of God to offer yourselves as a sacrifice, holy and pleasing to God, your spiritual service."

This is the true Christian spiritual life—to be made conformable to Christ, Priest and Victim, and it can come about only through an "active and conscious participation" in the Sacrifice of Christ offered in the Church. It is the very life of the holy People of God, the *Plebs Sancta*, of the Whole Body of Christ, and so, of each one of the members of that Body. Everyone who has been inserted into the Body of Christ by Baptism has received the seed of that life and is called to bring that seed to full blossoming, to greater development. Rightly viewed, the Christian life is a sacramental life and therefore a liturgical life.

When this essay was first projected, the schema on the liturgy placed before the Second Vatican Council was as yet unavailable in any form to the public. But since then Father Cipriano Vagaggini's summary of the main principles of the liturgy reform have become known to everyone. As a result we are provided now with an authoritative program of liturgical formation far exceeding any that we have had hitherto. Here we find clearly stated not only the norms that are to govern liturgical reform but especially the norms that should preside over the liturgical formation of the candidates for the priesthood. Much of what will be said in the course of this essay would have been said in any case—the principles guiding it have long been accepted in the Church. But given the fact that lawful authority has emphasized them anew and given them new expression, our study must necessarily be little more than a commentary on what is in the schema, coupled with a summary of suggestions that will help us to realize the provisions of that schema more effectively.

It should be obvious that we are now standing at the beginning of a new era in the life of the Church and of seminary training. What was adequate and sufficient even fifteen years ago is no longer adequate today; and the Council seems to sense that nothing short of a complete revolution in our procedure is going to meet the demands of the times we are living in. If people will not listen to us in one language, we have to talk to them in another; if they cannot be reached by one method, they have to be reached by another. The basic principles can never change, no more than the Church herself can change in her essential being. The priest in any age must be the man of God, the man of prayer, the apostle of the Gospel of Jesus Christ. But the way he is to be prepared to fulfill his apostolate must take into account the conditions of the world that he is going to live and work in.

The aspect of the pastoral office has changed greatly

during the past twenty-five years. Currents of thought and
movements of every kind have manifested themselves in
the life of the Church. Of all these movements none is
more significant than the liturgical revival and that other
which touches it so closely, the biblical revival. We have
long since learned to see that the liturgical revival is not the
archeological and archeologizing concern for the externals
of worship that it appeared to be in the far-off days before
and after the First World War. Now grown and still developing all the time, it emerges as a full-scale revival that
has its roots deep in the mystery of salvation and that represents an enormous quickening of the interior life of
the Church. Pius XII did not hesitate to say that it was
nothing less than "the passage of the Holy Spirit in the
Church."

It is not enough to know the liturgy from outside, we
must be aware of the riches within and be aware of its value
and its pastoral importance. The success of the liturgical
renewal depends almost exclusively upon the clergy, for if
the clergy do not receive the best possible formation in the
seminary, all our efforts will be in vain.

Only an enlightened and interested clergy can make all
this effective. If they are not solidly behind the liturgical
reforms, if they do not understand them and sympathize
with them, there can be no hope of success. We can go
no further and say that if priests are not turned in this direction during their seminary days, there is little likelihood
that they will ever be.

The first aim of the diocesan seminary is to prepare
priests for the pastoral ministry in the diocese they are ordained for. Now, as we have seen, the pastoral ministry

itself means, in fact, the building of the Church by bring-
in people into life-giving contact with the mystery of Christ.
This is done by introducing people into the liturgical
mysteries and making them into a living Christian community. This mission of the priest demands that he himself be formed to penetrate the mystery of Christ and to
live the liturgical life of the Church if he is to bring others
to live it.

But this is where the seminary comes in. Most candidates
for the priesthood do not look upon the liturgy as "the
primary and indispensable source of the true Christian
spirit." The object of liturgical formation is to do something effective about changing this situation—to show the
student what the liturgy is, first of all, and why it is important to live the liturgical life and to be imbued with
the liturgical spirit.

We introduce them into the liturgical life in two ways,
intimately connected with one another, and both equally
essential to our ultimate purpose: by giving them the theory
and by providing them with the practice. The first is done
in spiritual conferences and classes, the second is done by
the celebration of the liturgy.

Since, as we have said, the liturgy is above all and primarily a life to be lived, the first instrument of a solid, lasting
and profound liturgical formation is the sacred rites themselves. It is they that constitute the liturgy; it is they that
are the source and summit that the Council speaks of. The
liturgy is not just something we talk about or read about,
it is primarily something done—an action.

The importance of the liturgy in the life of the Church
and so its importance in the formation of the candidate for

the priesthood can only be grasped when we understand
what the liturgy is. The schema on the liturgy drawn up for
the Council begins by establishing its doctrinal basis. The
liturgy flows from the nature and work of Christ. He is
Himself the first, the original "sacrament," *sacramentum,
mysterium,* basic to all worship and all sanctification. From
this first-born *sacramentum* comes the sacrament which is
the Church herself (*totius Ecclesiae tuae mirabile sacramentum*) which was born from the side of Christ that it
might apply the work of the redemption to men. This work
of Redemption is carried on by the Church first of all by
the Holy Sacrifice and the other sacraments around which
the whole liturgy is developed—always, as with Christ himself, in an incarnational and sacramental structure. In the
words of the schema again, the liturgy appears "as the
exercise of the priesthood of Christ in Whom by means of
sacred signs the sanctification of man is communicated and,
in the manner proper to each [sign], brought about; and,
at the same time, the Mystical Body of Christ, Head and
members, offers the entire public worship."

As a result of this dogmatic fact, the liturgy is seen as
"the summit toward which all the actions of the Church
tend and at the same time the source from which it derives all its strength." Consequently, the Church is anxious
to bring to the people and to live intensely such a treasure;
she is preoccupied with seeing that the clergy is fully instructed, otherwise this spirit cannot be passed on to the
faithful.

We have here, it seems, the blueprint for the liturgical
formation of the future priest. Every seminary should provide a full and complete liturgical life. Anything less than

this is to ignore the plain wishes of the Church. It isn't a question of the liturgy being made everything or of its "taking over" the seminary. It *is* a matter of giving the celebration of the liturgy the place that it should have in the life of the seminary. Everything that any other practice or practices can contribute to the formation of the future priest can be obtained just as well and better by the celebration of the liturgy, *provided* that it is done properly and above all made to be a real, living, experience.

"Readily provide the young clerical student with facilities to understand the sacred rites, to appreciate their majesty and beauty and to learn the rubrics with care," just as you do when he is trained in ascetics, in dogma and in canon law and pastoral theology. This should not be done merely for cultural reasons, and to fit the student to perform religious rites in the future, correctly and with due dignity, but *especially to lead him into closest union with Christ the Priest so that he may become a holy minister of sanctity.*

"Providing them with facilities to understand" is a more elaborate way of saying "let him take part in the celebration of the sacred mysteries"—providing him with the opportunity to live a full liturgical life. In practice this means first of all that the Mass is, even in its outward rite, made to appear as the chief action of the day. Besides the Mass there should be daily recitation of some portions of the Office and, finally, the reverent observance of those extraordinary rituals during the year (like the Candlemas procession, for example). In other words, the seminary should provide the full liturgical life of the Church—everything that should be done in parish churches. To put it briefly, the celebration of the liturgy should be the center of the life of the seminary. Everything else should radiate from it or be influenced by it and in turn refer back to it.

This is a good place to say that the success of the liturgical program in any seminary depends upon the active cooperation of the whole seminary staff. It must appear as the *official attitude* of the seminary itself and not as the special activity of a few. This has perhaps been the chief trouble with our formation in the past—a few men on the faculty talked about these things and the rest did not. Inevitably, therefore, the students got the idea that all this was very interesting perhaps, but not really essential—that one could get along without it.

The object of the liturgical life in the seminary is to make the students enter deeply into the life of the Church, and to teach them to make the people enter into this same life. The liturgy is not merely an ecclesiastical science that can be adequately taught in a classroom, it is, above all, a *life* and life has to be lived. The Liturgy is in a class by itself in this respect: it is, as the name indicates (l[e]it-urgy— from the Greek *ergon*—a work, a deed) an action, a deed, something that is *done*. It is an ensemble of words and acts that go to make up a sacred action done by the People of God, the Church. The reality embraced by the word is not primarily a reality of the speculative order; though it can become the object of speculation and reflection, it belongs to the practical order. From this it follows that the first emphasis in liturgical formation must be placed not on instruction, but on doing the liturgy, on the celebration of the Sacred Mysteries and living the liturgical life. The Liturgy can really only be learned by those who are living it. The liturgical spirit is certainly not something that can be learned in a classroom; it demands a setting in which it can take hold and grow and develop.

The liturgy well celebrated is the greatest instrument of a sound liturgical education, even though this is not the first purpose of the celebration itself. When we say the liturgy "well celebrated," we mean not simply the fulfilling the letter of the law—having a High Mass on Sundays and Feast Days or a dialogue Mass on weekdays, still less, needless to say, do we have in mind only the "correct performance" of "the ceremonies" (as people used to speak of the liturgy in pre-*Mediator Dei* times), but a whole well-integrated and developed program of celebration.

No preparation for the sacred priesthood can take the place of a solid initiation into the mystery of Christ the Priest by constant and reflective practice of the liturgy of the Church. The seminary should teach the seminarian that his spiritual life has its source in the Mass and the Office. It isn't enough to *tell* him this. The very life of the seminary should *proclaim* this to him by the importance it gives to the proper devout and reflective celebration of the Mass and the recitation of at least some of the hours of the Breviary. It will do little good to say with Pius XII that "the most important duty of priest and people is to live the liturgical life and to be penetrated with the liturgical spirit" if in practice other things are made to appear more important than the liturgical services of the Church. The practice of the seminary should not contradict the theory.

The day of liturgical pomp and baroque splendor is long past and gone; and we should be grateful that it is. Hardly anything—except the utter absence of interior devotion—is more inimical to true worship than the showy or the

theatrical in any of its forms. Neither the music nor the ceremonies exist for their own sake, and a certain austere re-
straint in these matters is imperative, unless we want to see
the one or the other becoming the principal concern. At all
times, we must insist upon the absolute primacy of the
celebration itself.

The full liturgical life—adapted of course to its milieu—
should be found in the seminary no less than in the best
Benedictine monastery in the land. The daily community
Mass need not be a high Mass, though that is the ideal; but
it should always be *festive,* a real community celebration of
the Paschal Mystery daily made present in our midst. This
festive note can be sounded in various ways, for example by
singing hymns or psalms in the vernacular at the times when
they are permitted. It should not be necessary so long after
the Instruction of 1958 to say that all community Masses
should be dialogue Masses. The seminarian cannot begin
too early in his career to learn the great lesson of the modern
liturgical revival: that the Mass is a sacred community action in which all are to take full part according to their position in the Church. Of course, this participation must
always be first of all an *interior* participation. This might be
a good place to remark that while no individual is compelled
to participate outwardly and vocally and there is more than
one way of taking part in the Mass, the best way is the
Church's way: joining in the celebration with heart and
mind *and voice.*

Minor seminarians will need to be introduced into the
meaning of the texts of the Mass through a well-prepared
commentary that unfolds the meaning of the texts and
serves to make the readings, chants, and prayers more fruitful and effective.

No celebration of the Eucharist is complete without a homily, however brief. It is a vital part of the liturgical action; it is itself a liturgical action and thus it is a *sacramental* action and produces grace in a way that mere speaking outside the time of the liturgy does not produce and should, therefore, take precedence over any other form of oral communication. The homily should be given by celebrant because of the intrinsic link between the two actions —the breaking of the Bread of Life and the breaking of the Bread of the Word. They form together that nourishment which "the faithful and wise servant whom the Lord has placed over his household" is called upon to "give the Lord's family in due season."

The liturgy is the consecrated place for the proclamation of the Word of God. The first part of the Mass is a true celebration of the Word in which the saving mystery of Christ which becomes present in the Eucharistic sacrifice is heralded to the congregation. The hearing of the Word of God is the first purpose of the liturgical assembly.

This is hardly the place to go into a full development of the theology of the Word and its place in the liturgical celebration. All we have time for is to recall the basic principle and to point out how its application is to be made in the context of the seminary celebration of the liturgy.

The celebration of the liturgy in the seminary should be as full and complete as possible. Whatever the liturgical renewal seeks to bring about in the parish situation should be done in the seminary. A case in point is the matter of giving Communion from hosts consecrated at *this* Mass. Otherwise and inevitably, the idea that Communion is a *sharing* in *this* Sacrifice will of necessity be obscured. To bring out the relationship between Mass and Communion and to ensure that Communion will be given with hosts consecrated at each Mass, some kind of Offertory procession would seem desirable. There are ways of doing this that would not take up much time yet would underline the basic idea that the Offertory procession seeks to express that in the Mass we give or offer *ourselves* under the symbol of the bread, which is consecrated and given back to us as the Body of Christ.

The daily Mass during the first session of the Second Vatican Council was celebrated upon an altar facing the assembly. Many of those who were present have spoken of the deep impression that Mass said in this way made upon them. Far from being odd or strange, it seemed to be the most natural thing in the world. It promotes participation and gives a sense of union with the Mass action in a way that the more usual form of celebrating does not. The contact between celebrant and congregation is more easily established and maintained by this practice. It seems imperative that this way of celebrating Mass should be followed in the seminary, at least from time to time. The obvious benefits to be derived from this practice; the fact that it makes the Mass more meaningful, that it gives a sense of participating in the common action of the Church, that we are truly *circumstantes*, should be sufficient inducement to do this in a seminary.

Let us hope that the new emphasis on the liturgical formation in the seminary will inspire us to have the seminarians receive Communion at the High Mass on Sundays and Feast Days. This is certainly more in keeping with the spirit of the liturgy than the usual practice of having the students receive at one Mass earlier in the morning and then coming back later on to a Solemn Mass without Communion. To separate Communion from the Mass in that way is unreal, because everything that is done at High Mass is to bring out the corporate community character of the Eucharist. Without Communion the Solemn Mass will inevitably take on the aspect of a liturgical "function," a show. It is no wonder that students find it so difficult to take part in such a Mass with any real devotion. For each man, the true Mass of the day is the Mass at which he goes to Communion, and another Mass (when it is a High Mass) seems burdensome to him. There should be only one *community* Mass on Sunday, the High Mass.

Besides forming the seminarian in the Christian life and virtues, the great ruling object of the liturgical training should be to form celebrants, to give them the mentality and outlook of celebrants: *oportet sacerdotem praeesse.* He should be constantly aware of his role as president of the liturgical assembly. When he celebrates the Sacred Mysteries, he is not engaged in private devotion but is leading the People of God in worship. This celebrant's instinct is not something that one comes by naturally; it can only be acquired by thorough instruction and much practice. The instruction will be given by means of a solid grounding in the theology of the Assembly; the practice can be given only in the actual liturgical assembly itself.

A most necessary part of the liturgical formation of future priests will, therefore, be training in the careful, exact and reverent celebration of the liturgy according to the rules laid down in the liturgical books. At the same time it is only fair to say that seminarians should have a relaxed attitude toward ceremonial. The sanctuary should not have the atmosphere of the parade ground, nor should the ceremonial actions resemble a military drill. The "court ceremonial" and "sacred etiquette" approach to the liturgy is, or should be, a thing of the past, otherwise no one will believe that the liturgy is the primary and indispensable source of the true Christian spirit.

As always happens in times of change and adjustment, there have been and still are people who are restless and impatient with authority. Young people are particularly prone to this sort of thing. But, as often as not they provoke a reaction that puts roadblocks in the path of the true liturgical apostolate.

Closely allied to this is what we might call the party spirit, which prompts some to look down their noses at the devotional practices of the Church and to speak disparagingly of those who are not as enlightened in these matters as they fancy themselves to be. What it amounts to often is a kind of neo-Gnosticism. Students, whatever their feelings may be about devotional practices that other people indulge in, must respect the liberty and the dignity of these people. Aside from the fact that this is only good manners, it is demanded by the very liturgical life they profess to lead. Nothing is more foreign to the whole idea of the liturgy than the spirit of independence carried to excess.

The great characteristic of our times is what can be called the re-discovery of the Church as a living community. Everything about the Church, even spirituality, has taken on an ecclesial dimension; we are becoming more and more conscious of the fact that we are not alone. Spirituality is no longer seen as an isolated spiritual combat but as a life lived in and with the Church. It calls for a true and constant inward assimilation to Christ, putting on Christ and identification with Him. It is the full committal and perfect surrender of the whole man to Christ, is lived in the context of the Church, the Body of Christ and His mysterious extension. It is the life of Christ lived over in us through the action of the Holy Spirit.

This new awareness of the Chruch as a community of life in the Holy Spirit must be given expression in the seminary. The seminary community must be seen as it really is: the local expression of the world-wide community of the faithful that is the Catholic Church. Thus the Divine Office should find proper place in the daily life of the seminaries, for it is not simply the private prayer of the priest, it is the prayer of the whole Church. By giving the daily recitation of the Office an honored place in the life of the seminarian we enable him to enter into the current of the prayer of the Church and so foster the ecclesial spirit, the spirit of community, the awareness of belonging to a community, the Body of Christ.

Next to the Mass, it is his *sacrificium laudis*, the concrete response to the exhortation of the Epistle to the Hebrews: "Let us ever offer the victim of praise to the Lord, that is, the fruit of lips praising his name" (Heb 13:15).

Some seminaries have adopted the practice of daily Prime and Compline, others Lauds and Compline. Perhaps a better choice would be Lauds for morning prayers and Vespers for evening prayers. Both Lauds and Vespers follow more closely the rhythm of the liturgical year; they are the oldest hours of the Office and originated among the people. They form the true morning and evening prayer of the Church, they reflect the nature of the Church as the People of God better. It may be that the future revision of the Breviary will settle this question, as well as others, by making a new arrangement of morning and evening prayers.

The sacred rites have a power inherent in themselves to sanctify and perfect, but they are not magic formulas. To the *ex opere operato* must be added the *ex opere operantis*. This is the constant teaching of the Church and it is expressed in the texts of the liturgy itself: *Quod ore sumpsimus pura mente capiamus*. It is an illusion to think that the sole celebration of the sacred rites will of itself sanctify us. The liturgy presupposes preparation and that preparation is prayer. To think that all we have to do is to take part in the liturgy is sheer liturgism. Hence, the absolute necessity of meditation and private prayer during the day and especially before we enter upon any liturgical act. Of their very nature the liturgical acts do not permit any extensive pauses while they are being celebrated; this very fact indicates that the normal food for meditation and prayer outside the liturgy should be the Missal and the Breviary and, of course, the Bible. In them he can truly learn to realize what he is doing. In this way, the mystery of Christ which he celebrates at the altar he will contemplate with love and devotion outside the time of the liturgical celebration.

The celebration of the Sacred liturgy must be an intelligent celebration. The liturgy is never self-evident; it requires a thorough catechesis before we can take a full and understanding part in it. The history of the liturgy shows that from ancient times its celebration was always either accompanied or preceded by a "mystagogy," a catechesis designed to introduce the faithful or the catechumen into the understanding of the mystery. The writings of the Fathers of the

Church contain much evidence of this preoccupation on the part of the Church.

It requires no small biblical culture to appreciate the Psalms, for example, and their place in the prayer-life of the Church. To impart this necessary culture should be one of the main objects of the seminary faculty. This means that not only the formal classes in Scripture and liturgy must be orientated toward imparting this culture but what those in charge of the spiritual formation of the students—whether the spiritual director or the rector—should point out the great themes of the psalter and show the relation of the psalms to the spiritual life.

What we have said about the psalms is only by way of example. Needless to say, it applies to the liturgy as a whole. The spiritual conference on Saturday night should be an introduction to the main themes of the next day's celebration, so that the students may be prepared to take an intelligent part in the Sunday Mass and Vespers. There can be no intelligent participation of the faithful in the liturgy without an initiation into the mystery. Precisely because it is a mystery it is accessible only to the faith and, therefore, postulates a catechesis that is "a living and praying initiation which begins from the rites themselves in order to clarify them and has for its object to make the faithful enter into the mystery of worship" (A. T. Martimort, *L'Église en Prière* [Desclée, 1961], p. 289). Any kinds of catechesis will not do. It must not be a dry, lifeless explanation of the sacred rites, but rather it should be stimulating and inspiring, drawn from the *conferencier's* own experience of having lived the mysteries he is explaining. Naturally, such a catechesis is impossible to give without serious study, but, above all, it must come from one who is *himself* living the mysteries that he is explaining. What he says must be a part of him, the fruit of his contemplation. St. Gregory the Great says that every pastor must be a contemplative: he must live in and by the mysteries he celebrates and proclaims to others.

The celebration of the Church year should have a large place in the life of the seminary community. The various feasts and seasons should be prepared for by conferences, reading, Bible-vigils. The students should be introduced to Advent and Christmas, Lent, Holy Week, Easter, Pentecost gradually and shown their great themes and their significance for the spiritual life. The Paschal Mystery, the *Transitus Domini*, our Lord's Passage to His Father through His Death and Resurrection-Ascension and our passage with Him is the great central theme of the Christian life. It should be the great center of the spirituality of the priest and the candidate for the priesthood. Every conference and every instruction should be centered upon it; it should permeate all our teaching, as the schema of the Second Vatican Council directs: "Integrate the mystery of Christ and salvation history into each subject." This should be done all through the year; it should not be confined only to Lent and Holy Week. The message is the same for all time; it is only sounded louder during this season. The Mass is the daily celebration of the Paschal Mystery. To enter into this daily celebration we must live with this mystery the whole year round. Only on that condition, can we come to the full understanding of what the Christian life is—a daily dying and rising with Christ.

Once this has been made clear we are free to say that

Lent and Holy Week and Eastertime are the very sancutary of the celebration of this one great Mystery.

The second means of liturgical formation is the teaching of liturgy as a science. Here again we have directions from the Vatican Council. From now on liturgy will no longer be an auxiliary subject in seminary curriculum; it is to take its place among the major seminary disciplines. The Council envisages that it will be a solid, complete and profound study that neglects no aspect of the science. It is to be taught "from a theological and historical aspect, as well as from a spiritual, pastoral and juridical aspect." Too often in the past the course in liturgy has been a course in rubrics, or perhaps a course in the history of the liturgy. This has been true partly because we have had only incomplete, one-sided, or perhaps even erroneous, ideas about what the liturgy is. Now that the true concept of the liturgy has been clarified for us by the Holy See and the great theologians of the liturgy, we no longer have any excuse for one-sided and in-complete presentations of the subject. The insistence upon teaching the pastoral aspect is significant; it is safe to say that this is to be the guiding norm of the whole study and teaching of liturgy in the future. Once the principle is estab-lished, as it is, that the liturgy is primarily *pastoral*, that it is "the *summit* toward which all the actions of the Church tend and at the same time the *source* from which it draws all its strength," everything else in the course of liturgical study falls into line. The study of history is necessary to clarify our understanding of the nature and the purpose of the various rites to see what role they have played in the past and the causes that have prevented them from attain-ing their full object. The study of liturgical theology is necessary so that we may grasp the meaning and the effect as well as the content of these same sacred rites.

The spirituality of the liturgy will show the place of the liturgy in the devotional life. Liturgical law will play the role of preserving a right sense of the authority of the Church in the regulation of the liturgy.

Another significant provision of the schema is the recommendation that the professors of the other theological disciplines, especially of dogmatic, spiritual, and pastoral theology, integrate into each subject the mystery of Christ and salvation history so that the lines of relation can be clearly seen between each other branch and the liturgy, for *greater realization of unity in priestly formation.* Too often in the past, liturgy has been isolated even from the other theological disciplines by the fact that another language than that used by theologians of the liturgy has been used in the other classes. In presenting the great themes of the liturgy, the liturgical theologians have at times had to seem to contradict what was taught in other classes. The view of the redemption, of grace, the sacraments, that the liturgy enshrines in prayers seems to be at variance with the views of some of the schools of theology. The liturgy is biblical rather than scholastic in its way of looking at the mystery of Christ. It prefers salvation history to theological analysis and so can appear to suffer by comparison with the careful language of the schools. Without in any way sacrificing the benefits of the scholastic presentation, the dogma professors can show that the view of redemption or graces or the sacraments that we find expressed in the prayer-forms of the liturgy is in line with the view of the Scriptures and the Fathers.

It should not be necessary for those who are teaching liturgy to have to defend the ideas that are presented in the liturgy or to vindicate them from the charge of vagueness or imprecision simply because they don't use the language or follow the categories of scholasticism. The liturgy is doctrine, but doctrine is expressed in prayer-form rather than in strictly theological language.

What is particularly welcome about this part of the schema is that it takes a long stride toward a genuine integration of theological studies. Needless to say, the whole tone of the schema effectively discourages the irresponsible criticism which sometimes during the past twenty-five years has confused and bewildered students and made for misunderstanding and disunity.

The provisions of the schema on the teaching of the liturgy call for a complete revision of the liturgy course. The details of a truly comprehensive liturgy course that will meet the desires of the Council are still to be worked out. All we can hope to do in an essay of this kind is to indicate the broad outlines that such a course should follow and the principles that should govern its presentation. We suppose in what follows that liturgy will be assigned the number of hours that is given now to the other major disciplines in the seminary curriculum.

Without minimizing or belittling the other seminary disciplines, we will have to maintain that this course is unlike almost any other—not better or superior but *unlike* any other—in that it touches most closely upon the future life of the candidate for the priesthood. Its aims and objectives must, therefore, be primarily and even almost wholly *pastoral* because it is intended to prepare him to enter more fully into the understanding of the liturgy so that he may take part in it more effectively. Like the celebration of the sacred rites, the liturgy course must keep these two objects in mind all the time.

The subject of the study of liturgy is nothing less than the life of the Church in action, as we have seen. It would seem then, that it must have its own method, altogether different from other subjects. The primary textbook of the liturgy course must be the very texts of the liturgy itself: the Missal, the Breviary, the Ritual, the Pontifical.

Just as the Scripture course should not be only a study about the Bible without ever looking at the text of the Scriptures, so a course in liturgy should not be primarily *about* the liturgy but *on* the liturgy, a study of the liturgy itself as it is. The real work of the liturgy professor is to be a *mystagogus*, to initiate students into the mystery by opening up the text and showing them what is in it and what it means.

A manual can be of service here, but mostly as a reference tool. It can never take the place of the official texts themselves. The first principle must always be that a good liturgy course must be a commentary, doctrinal, historical, devotional, pastoral, upon the texts themselves; but upon the texts as they are going to be used in the celebration of the liturgy, in the context of the whole sacred rite itself. A study of the Canon of the Mass, for example, should as much as possible be made in the context of the actual celebration of the Mass because it really comes to life only in that context. It should be above all approached as a prayer, as the Great Eucharistic Prayer, the Prayer of Consecration, that is, the very heart of the Mass itself. And it should be approached, as it were, in the act of its being recited with all the dimensions and resonances that it acquires in the very act itself. The Scripture texts used in the liturgy should be studied *in situ*, that is, not only what they mean in themselves but what they mean in the context of this or that sacred rite. This method is the only living method of studying the liturgy; it is observing it in action, with all the vigor and force and life that action has.

This is the absolutely indispensable criterion of the excellence of a seminary liturgy course. Our purpose is not to prepare historians, or masters of ceremonies, or savants, but *parish priests* who are going to exercise the pastoral ministry chiefly through the liturgical rites. The better they understand them and the more they love them and, above all, live by them, the better they will fulfill their functions as ministers of the New Covenant. The first task of the professor of liturgy is to explain the liturgical books, not as historical documents but as the store-houses of redemptive life; in other words, as living beings rather than collections of facts.

The formal liturgy course should begin with a thorough introduction to the fundamentals of the liturgy. Because it is fundamental, no time should be lost in giving it—at the latest in first year of theology. Only an hour a week would be enough, but it is indispensable. To wait until third year theology to introduce students formally to what they are doing from the first hour they set foot in the seminary doesn't make sense. Their progressive indoctrination in the liturgy should keep pace with their practice of it.

The introduction will, of course, deal with the nature of the liturgy itself, as the carrying out *in mysterio* and *in sacramento* of the work of the Redemption, the sacrifice and the sacraments as acts of Christ, the priesthood and the episcopate as sharing in the unique priesthood of Christ. Above all, it must always be an initiation into the Paschal

Mystery considered in all its dimensions: the *Transitus Domini*, event, rite, feast.

There will be no question in all of this of going into the special domain of the other courses. The liturgy course should not be a Scripture course or a dogma course, but solely and exclusively a course in the theology of the liturgy, touching upon these other points only so much as will be needed to help them understand the liturgy which, since it is dogma prayed, presupposes some knowledge of the various doctrines involved. There is all the difference in the world between showing the relevancy of the doctrine of the Redemption to the celebration of Mass, let us say, and giving a thorough course on the dogma of the Redemption itself.

An introduction to the liturgy should be largely a theology of the liturgy, beginning with the definition of the liturgy and an examination of the full meaning of the definition and an analysis of its parts. This will involve a study of the true nature of the Church as the People of God and the Body of Christ, in particular the notion of the Assembly, of the economy of salvation and so of the history of salvation. It will mean studying the great themes of salvation history, the Covenant, the Promises, the Exodus, Israel, the Temple and its worship, the Restoration, the Messianic Hope, the Messianic Reign, the life, teachings and miracles of Jesus, His death, resurrection and ascension.

This will also mean recalling the great figures of Old Testament times who were the types and the forerunners of Christ: Abraham, Moses, David, Joshua. The concrete themes of the Bible and the liturgy should not be neglected: Jerusalem, Israel, the Temple, the Lamb, the Shepherd, the Exodus, Mt. Sinai. The reason is that the liturgy is pervaded from beginning to end with these themes and concepts. We can never hope to make sense out of the Divine Office for example, if we don't see that the greater part of it is a vast compendium in song of salvation history.

Some explanation of the relation between public and private prayer should be given though a deeper study of this belongs to a course in ascetics or spirituality. Failure to appreciate the relation is one reason why so many priests never grasp the obvious fact that the Office is a prayer and a prayer meant to be said in common.

Once the ground has been cleared and the foundation laid by a course such as we have described, the seminary can go on to construct a solid program of liturgical studies. The way this will be done will vary, of course, and again we cannot hope to do more here than to indicate possibilities. Naturally there will be courses on the Mass, the Office, the Liturgical Year, the Sacraments.

The Mass can be approached as a whole, following the treatment given to it by Jungmann in his *Missarum Solemnia* (*The Mass of the Roman Rite*). It is not necessary, nor is it advisable, to treat all the *details* in class; these should be left to the student to fill in by outside reading. This is one place where a good manual is indispensable. The professor should indicate the general principles and the great themes of the Missal emphasizing the content of introit, collect, epistle and so forth. In short, his class will be a commentary on the text of the Missal itself, the meaning of the various parts of the Mass, the role of the introit, the gradual, the communion antiphon, the great themes of the Sunday and Feast Day Masses. He should explain the purpose of the first part of the Mass as the Liturgy of the Word and underscore the relationship of this to the Eucharistic Sacrifice that follows. It should be seen as a true celebration of the Word of God; it has its own end which is to proclaim the *mirabilia Dei* and to celebrate them. It is not a mere preparation but an independent part of the total Eucharistic rite.

Any study of the Mass should, of course, include the Canon, the Great Eucharistic Prayer, heart and center of the Mass. Here again we should not get lost in the details, but set forth the great themes and fill in the scriptural background so as to open it up to the students and reveal the treasures it contains. It should be presented to them in such a way that all its associations and implications will come through to them when they stand at the altar and that they will be inspired to take it up and read it and meditate upon it often during the course of their priestly lives.

Some place might be given in the course on the Mass to the projects for the reform of the Mass rite and the revision of the Missal. The professor could give the principles that should govern any genuine reform, and showing why reform is necessary and what it hopes to achieve.

The study of the Divine Office should, first of all, be a study of the theology of the Office, of its origin and development, the spirit of the hours, and the purpose of the elements that go to make it up, the main themes of the Psalter, and especially the Christian interpretation of the Psalms. Here too the projects for reform and the reasons behind them might be studied with profit.

The course on the liturgy of the sacraments should be a commentary on the Ritual or Pontifical, with enough of the history of the various rites to make them comprehensible. An adequate treatment of Baptism would have to include not only the study of the present Ritual but also the texts of the Lenten Masses that have a bearing on baptism; the liturgy of the Easter Vigil which is, in origin and content, very strongly oriented toward baptism, and in that Vigil, especially the blessing of the baptismal water; and finally, the baptismal texts of the Masses of Easter Week. Only against this background can we hope to grasp the full bearing of the baptismal mystery itself. Confirmation too has to be studied in relation to baptism and against the background of the Easter Vigil, because, as our present very brief confirmation rite shows, this sacrament was always given immediately after baptism and in the framework of the Easter Vigil.

The study of the Liturgical Year should be centered around the Paschal Mystery and the celebration of Easter. It should begin with the theology of the Liturgical Year and show that the principal object of the Liturgical Year is the celebration of the Mystery of Christ in all its dimensions: the Incarnation, the Life, Death and Resurrection of Christ. It will include, therefore, Advent and the Christmas–Epiphany cycle, Lent and Easter, the Easter Season and Pentecost, the time after Pentecost, the celebration of the Sunday as the weekly Easter, the Feast of All Saints, the chief Marian feasts and, if possible, the commemorations of the martyrs and other saints. As with the other sections of the course, the history and historical development of the feasts and seasons will have to be brought in to throw light upon the present celebration, but the chief emphasis should be placed upon the theology of the feasts and seasons, their spiritual and devotional content.

The relationship between the Liturgical Year and the ministry of preaching the Word should be constantly brought out during this study. We are coming more and more to see that our preaching should normally be a homily upon the texts of the Mass. In fact, the schema of the Council gives new emphasis to these homilies. The relationship between preaching and the liturgy is obvious enough; we are to proclaim in the pulpit what we celebrate at the altar, the Mystery of Christ.

Once these main elements have been provided for, the great sacramentals, like the Dedication of Churches, could be studied in greater detail. This would be a good place to consider the externals of the liturgy, the church edifice and its appointments, sacred art and decoration of the altar, the pulpit, arrangement of the sanctuary, the vestments, the sacred vessels. On the whole, it is better to consider these matters in the setting of the rite of the Dedication of Churches, so that they do not appear as detached and independent realities, but as subordinate to the end they are supposed to serve. This approach has the advantage of putting them in their proper and rightful place, so that they are never allowed to usurp the attention that should be given to the liturgy itself.

It is a fact that, wherever the true understanding of the liturgy prevails, the accessories and the setting of the liturgy will take care of themselves. We see instinctively that they should be fit for their purpose—simple, dignified and altogether worthy of the task they are called to fulfill. It hardly becomes necessary to insist on this where the full liturgical life is being lived.

On the other hand, too much insistence upon the cut of the chasuble, the use of linen for albs, or the outward splendor of worship, can give people the impression that this is what liturgy is really pre-occupied with. The externals of worship should be approached from the theological point of view, with a view to their role as aids to worship rather than as independent objects of study. In the same way, the rubrical details—the manner of reciting the Office, for example—should not be allowed to take up time that could be more profitably spent on the spirit and content of the liturgical texts.

Nevertheless the training of the clergy in good taste has its own importance and should have some place. It is far more related to the authentic worship of God than many are disposed to admit. The priest need not be an artist or an architect but he should have some idea of what is good and true and beautiful and in keeping with the spirit of prayer and worship. At the same time he should be able to recognize at once what is bad and false and ugly, whatever is mean, poor, vulgar and shoddy. He should have some sense of proportion and be able to see what has a place in the church and the sanctuary and what has not. A course in the fundamental canons of sacred art and in the pastoral requirements of a good church would be a welcome addition to any seminary curriculum.

Besides giving the future priest an understanding and a love of the liturgy and teaching him how to live the liturgical life, the seminary should prepare him to carry out the liturgical apostolate in the parish. This means that some time should be set aside to show him, for example, how to organize and set up the dialogue Mass, how to give a commentary, how to train others to be leaders and commentators, how to prepare and execute the proper celebration of Holy Week, how to hold Bible Vigils—in short, the management of the hundred and one details that a modern parish priest has to be concerned with. Just as he is taught how to celebrate Mass and how to baptize and how to preach and how to catechize he must also be taught how to lead the congregation in singing and praying and whatever has to be done to take participation take hold and be a success. This calls for a Liturgical Pastoral Theology. The right method of procedure in these matters is surely as important as being trained how to prepare marriage cases or how to keep books or raise funds.

To give a course such as we have outlined or anything like it obviously requires that we have professors who are competent. The day is past when anyone with a knowledge of rubrics and ceremonial could teach a satisfactory liturgy course. But we still are far from seeing that someone must be trained for teaching liturgy just as much as for dogma, moral or scripture. Perhaps the new rank bestowed on the study of liturgy will change all that.

What has been written in these pages is hardly more than an attempt to indicate the broad main outlines of the liturgical formation of future priests. A full-scale book would be needed to treat the subject adequately and completely.

Only an incurable optimist will think that the mere promulgation of conciliar legislation will, of itself, change existing situations or attitudes overnight. What has taken centuries to develop cannot possibly be done away with by a stroke of the pen. It will take years, maybe even decades before the impact of new legislation will be felt. The decrees of the Council open up the road we must travel. We can set out on that road now with confidence and hope knowing that by travelling along this road under the guidance of the Church and her liturgy we will reach the goal, which is the ever more perfect formation of the "minister of Christ and the dispenser of the mysteries of God."

6

Lectio divina and the Formation of the Modern Religious Woman

KATHRYN SULLIVAN, R.S.C.J.

The Sister Formation movement is the answer to a need, the expression of a hope, the pledge of a rich and fruitful future. The need is for religious women dedicated to excellence in their spiritual, professional and apostolic life. The hope is that communities working together will be able to provide a comprehensive training program furthering the religious formation, intellectual development, and specific purpose of members of every institute during postulancy, novitiate, juniorate, and post-profession years. That the pledge of success is in part already realized is evident to anyone who examines the achievements of the first ten years of the Sister Formation Conference.

A Decade of Progress

At the 1953 National Catholic Education Association Convention, Sister Mary Emil, I.H.M., of Marygrove College in Monroe, Michigan, proposed the establishment on a national basis of a Sister training program. This was envisaged as "an organization of Sisters and for Sisters." With the interest and support of Catholic school superintendents efforts were made during the year to discover to what extent religious communities were providing for the professional education of their members. The situation, it was learned, was far from ideal. A preliminary questionnaire addressed to 377 major superiors showed that only 13 of the 255 communities responding had programs in operation leading to a bachelor's degree. Replies from 118 institutes disclosed that they had no undergraduate facilities of their own and no easy access to suitably staffed Catholic colleges.

As a result of this survey the Executive Committee of NCEA established a Conference on Sister Formation and empowered it to set up regional conferences. The Conference did this and much more. Its achievements are reported in its publication, *The Sister Formation Bulletin*, edited by Sister Ritamary Bradley, C.H.M., of Ottumwa Heights College, Ottumwa, Iowa. Vision and realism have guided the leaders from the beginning. A grant from the Michael P. Grace Foundation made possible the publication of the regional conference papers. A $50,000 grant was secured from the Ford Foundation Fund for the Advancement of Education in order to support:

1. A research study of curriculum in the education of Sister teachers, to investigate:

   a. the strong points in content and methods of teacher-training among the various Sisterhoods,

   b. the direction in which the religious congregations themselves feel a need for change or improvement.

2. A curriculum construction project, in which there
   would be application of the data obtained above, to
   the actual drawing up of an ideal curriculum in pre-
   service Sister education on the bachelor's level,
   through the work of a committee of Sister educators
   and special consultants.

With the encouragement of Catholic leaders (Cardinal
Spellman had advanced money to begin the project even
before the grant was made) fifteen Sisters plus an equal
number of educator consultants spent three months con-
structing a tentative curriculum for the religious and professional training of Sisters. Conclusions reached at this meeting at Providence Hospital in Everett, Washington, were
then discussed at regional conferences. Adopting and adapting suggestions received from thousands of educators in
every part of the country, the Sister Formation leaders established two centers where this experimental program
could be demonstrated—one by the Sisters of Charity of
Providence in conjunction with the University of Seattle,
the other by the Sisters of St. Francis of Rochester, Minne-
sota, at St. Teresa's College in Winona.

The next important advance was made in 1957 when the
Rev. Emilio Gambari, S.M.M., a member of the Sacred
Congregation for Religious, prepared, at the request of the
Sister Formation Conference, a carefully articulated program for the spiritual training of Sisters from postulancy
through the juniorate. Basing his plan on papal directives,
he showed that their intellectual and spiritual advancement
of Sisters must move *pari passu*.

Convinced that there should be no dichotomy between

the spiritual and intellectual life, Sister Annette Walters, C.S.J., the present executive secretary of Sister Formation Conference, has been indefatigable in her efforts to integrate the training of religious during their pre-service and in-service years. Her work has carried her to many countries of Europe and South America. It embraces education in all its dimensions. Her aim can be summed up in the words of Archbishop Romolo Carboni:

> To achieve (your goal) requires faith, and integral Christian faith. It demands that the whole of your spirituality, your theological knowledge, your secular learning be caught up in the one living fire of adoration and charity; it requires that there be no series of isolated departments in your life: such as one for your spiritual devotion, another for your theological learning, a third for your endeavors to consecrate the things of the world, and so on. Each and every activity must be a unified integral part in the living faith, a forward movement of spiritual growth, Christian insight, apostolic effort and effective missionary endeavor (Sursum Corda, vol. 5, p. 244).

Among the many ways in which the Sister Formation leaders are working to achieve this goal should be mentioned the establishment of special institutes in ascetical theology and in the theology and practice of the vows. Here as elsewhere, Sister Annette's desire is for excellence. "Our goal is excellence," she affirms. Nothing short of excellence, should be the response of all those who are able to benefit from the new opportunities opening before them. Theirs should be no selfish, narrow aim. Religious women should therefore "use all their resources for the enrichment of America, increasing vocations and extending the Church's work of mercy throughout the world."

An educational program, no matter how brilliantly conceived and competently administered, is limited in its effects by the will-to-excellence of those educated. Skillful teachers can form and inform those they are training, but life tests the results of education, and those who do not possess within themselves the power for further development will disappoint both themselves and others.

Lectio divina in the Sixth Century

Is there one single instrument of formation that will ensure consistent, resourceful advance, and prevent a blunted purpose, decelerating pace, and myopic point of view? High on any list of factors indicating continuing growths must be placed reading. Nor is this a new idea in the Church. In the sixth century the hours of a normal Benedictine summer day were divided according to a pattern similar to this:

Opus Dei	3½ hours
Lectio divina	4½ hours
Manual labor	6½ hours
Sleep	8½ hours
Meals	1 hour

In winter the shorter days meant fewer hours for reading but in any season on Sundays, when manual labor ceased, the monks were expected to increase the number of hours devoted to reading.

During Lent those in the school of the Lord's service were enjoined to give themselves with renewed fervor to their search for God in His inspired word.

So important did St. Benedict believe this precept of sacred reading to be that he took disciplinary measures to safeguard its observance. Lest the slothful brother idle or gossip when his eyes should be on his manuscript and his lips sealed, two senior monks, *circatores*, were deputed to go round the monastery to observe, rebuke, and, if need be, report the wandering, the dozing, or the garrulous to the abbot.

What books were recommended by the Father of Monasticism? When he comes to the last paragraph of his rule he urges that those who are hastening towards their heavenly country should study three great classes of works. The first includes the Old and the New Testament. "For what page or what word is there in the divinely inspired books of the Old and New Testaments, that is not a most accurate rule for human life?" In order to understand the light-bringing and life-giving chapters of the Bible St. Benedict then recommends the eager searching of commentaries on Scripture written by the Fathers, because they "loudly proclaim how we may by a straight course reach our Creator." Lastly, he counsels the study of special works that contain the advice and the example of those who have fashioned their lives on the Word of God.

Fourteen centuries have passed since St. Benedict composed his rule but the principle of *lectio divina* is valid today. Great masters of the interior life have produced masterpieces of spiritual writing which can help souls to fulfill their own individual vocations, but the Christian ideal will never be fully realized unless the soul makes central the lessons of the one true master, the Word of God.

St. Caesarius of Arles in his *Statuta Sanctarum Virginum* (18–20) required his nuns to read Scripture for two hours each day. At their meals and when spinning they were to listen to passages of the Bible that were read aloud to them and when engaged in other work they were "always to ruminate something from Holy Scripture." The forceful word *ruminatio* recurs constantly in medieval pages. It indicates the slow and loving repetition of a text selected from Sacred Scripture, allowing the words to linger sweetly in the *os cordis*, or to use another term, difficult to translate, in the *palatum cordis*. This means the slow assimilation of the inner meaning of the inspired sentence by a kind of "chewing" that releases its hidden flavor and nourishes the soul.

William of St. Thierry calls this holy process "meditative prayer." Without it no spiritual progress is possible. With it no other reading is necessary. As Arnoul the Cistercian explained: "He who reads should seek for savor not for science. Sacred Scripture is the well of Jacob from which water is drawn that will be poured out later in prayer. No need to hasten to the church to pray, but reading itself becomes a praying and a seeing."

Caesarius reminded the holy women whom he was trying to lead heavenward that God spoke to them in many ways. Not only could they hear the divine Word during their *lectio divina* but when they were in church they were to pay special heed each time the Bible was read during liturgical services and to the whole psalter which they recited at the eight daily offices prescribed by St. Benedict.

The Bible in the Liturgy

To subtract the biblical riches contained in liturgical books would be to reduce Missal, Ritual, Pontifical and Breviary to a fraction of their present size and to strip them of grace-giving values. It would mean the loss of such passages of Scripture as are found in the Epistles, Gospels, the first nocturns of matins, many antiphons, etc., as well as in some of the prayers of the Mass and the formulae of other liturgical rites where the influence of the Bible is less evident but equally important. To give only four examples: the *Crux Fidelis* of Good Friday, the *Exsultet* of the Paschal Vigil, the *Victimae Paschali* of Easter, the *Sanctus* of every Mass.

Examples can be multiplied in the sacramental rites of the Roman liturgy, baptism, orders, marriage. This is also true of sacraments administered in Eastern Churches which are always celebrated in the context of a true liturgy of God's Word. In both East and West the whole Mass is a kerygma of the divine Word. It is a proclamation of the mystery of Christ: the saving intervention that had been prefigured in the Old Testament and has been realized in the New.

Much of the meaning of the mystery is lost on Christians today because of the lapse of the homily. The lessons enshrined in the liturgy need explanation now as they did when Rupert of Deutz wrote his prologue to a study of the liturgy:

> The rites which follow the yearly cycle in the divine office are symbols of the highest realities, they include the greatest sacraments and all the majesty of heavenly mysteries. They were instituted for the glory of the head of the Church, Our Lord Jesus Christ, by those who had plumbed the sublime meaning of the mysteries of His Incarnation, His Birth, His Passion, His Resurrection and His Ascension. Not only had they understood these truths but they possessed the power to explain them.... Among the spiritual gifts with which the Holy Spirit enriches His Church, we should lovingly cultivate the one which consists in the ability to understand what we say in prayer and psalmody.

The theology of preaching has received thoughtful study in recent years. There is a growing realization that the New Testament division of preaching into *kerygma* and *didache* is as valid today as it was in apostolic times. The proclamation of the good news of salvation achieved by God in Christ should be coupled with an explanation of the related dogmatic and moral lessons.

To receive this instruction requires an openness to God's grace, an enlightened faith, a hunger and thirst for eternal truth. To increase our own capacity and to prepare others to receive such instruction requires an approach to Sacred Scripture that is scientific, soundly theological and founded on all the advances made in the biblical field within the last fifty years.

Papal Directives

As Pius XII pointed out in his encyclical *Divino afflante Spiritu* at the beginning of this century "hardly a single place in Palestine had begun to be explored by means of relevant excavations." Such investigations are today commonplace, and what is of even greater importance, since then "more precise methods and technical skill have been developed in the course of actual experience, enabling us to secure information that is at once more abundant and more accurate." The value of these archeological surveys is enhanced by the discovery of "written documents which help much toward the knowledge of the languages, literature, events, customs, and forms of worship in ancient times."

The Holy Father does not hesitate to urge those who

wish to profit from their reading of Sacred Scripture to apply themselves diligently "to acquire daily a greater facility in biblical as well as in other Oriental languages and to support their interpretation by the aids which all branches of philology supply." While stressing the importance of the essential ancillary sciences, he never loses sight of the goal he envisages: that "all the faithful may be helped to lead a life that is holy and worthy of a Christian."

This insistence on a deeper understanding of biblical theology requires that the exegete "search out and expound the literal meaning of the words, intended and expressed by the sacred writer and that he do likewise for the spiritual sense, provided it is clearly intended by God." This is a serious responsibility and shows why a thorough grounding in biblical science is necessary for the profitable reading and trustworthy teaching of the Bible.

It is clear that *lectio divina* requires prudent and skillful preparatory studies. The encyclical *Humani generis* warns of deviations that the unwary may easily make unless they observe the wise moderation the Holy Father had recommended earlier. Only those will be safe from danger who are well-informed in sacred and profane sciences and who wish to know what God told us in the Sacred Letters rather than what an ingenious orator or writer may suggest by a clever use of the words of Scripture. Nor does "the word of God, living and effectual and more piercing than any two-edged sword and reaching unto the division of the soul and the spirit, of the joints also and the marrow, and a discerner of the thoughts and intents of the heart" (Heb 4:12) need artificial devices and human adaptation to move and impress souls; for the Sacred Pages, written under the inspiration of the Spirit of God, are of themselves rich in original meaning; endowed with a divine power, they have their own value; adorned with heavenly beauty, they radiate of themselves light and splendor, provided they are so fully and accurately explained by the interpreter, that all the treasures of wisdom and prudence, therein contained, are brought to light.

God's Divine Plan

Women religious who wish to read the Bible and to attain a new understanding of its divine treasures must disengage the pattern of divine love as it is expressed in sacred history. The value of every religion and every philosophy can be tested by the answers proposed in the ageless questions that perenially confront man: Can God and man meet? Does God care about man? Why must man suffer? The existentialist response that the ways of God and man are irreconcilable and that the search for human happiness is absurd, are refuted in the history of salvation that is unfolded in the Bible.

Kierkegaard liked to speak of "the eternal contemporaneity of Christ," in the same sense it is also correct to speak of the actuality of the biblical message. In it is recounted the story of God's love for man and man's slow and often faltering response. The historical and geographical setting for the search for the meaning of life belongs to earlier centuries and distant lands which are much unlike our own but there is a timeless quality about these ancient joys and sorrows, hopes and disappointments, anguish, loneliness, dread, and the constant warring of nation with nation that overshadows the few and fitful interludes of peace.

The Bible is a universe and to those who are untouched

by modern scientific biblical studies it may well seem a confused and confusing place. Bishop Burnet who died in 1715 could not hide similar misgivings about the unsymmetrical arrangement of the heavens. He dared to observe how sadly order was lacking in the arrangement of the heavenly bodies; he sighed: "What a beautiful hemisphere they would have made, if they had been placed in rank and order, if they had been dispersed in regular figures . . . all finished and made up into one fair piece of great composition according to rules of art and symmetry."

Twentieth-century astronauts could assure the anxious divine that there is an order in the heavens of which he never dreamed and today's exegete has made the same discovery in Scripture. He has carefully charted the course of God's plan for the salvation of man as it is recorded in the sacred books. Only the untrained could claim to be confused or find the plan of salvation confusing.

There are four great periods in this history. All four are rich in meaning. The story of salvation is the story of the covenant which begins with God's promises to Abraham. The patriarch was told that he would have many descendants, that these descendants would possess their own land, that through one of these descendants blessings would reach all men. Abraham believed and waited. His son, his grandson, his great-grandson held fast to their belief but centuries were to pass before Yahweh spoke again.

The stupendous deliverance of Abraham's many descendants from bondage in Egypt, the solemn covenant on Sinai, the patient years of training in the desert, were followed by the fulfillment of the second promise and the chosen people crossed the Jordan and entered their own land. Judges attempted to preserve some semblance of unity in a weak amphictyony as the people evolved from nomadic to simple forms of agricultural and urban life.

Three kings, Saul, David and Solomon, ruled over a small but swiftly growing kingdom. Apparently, God's plan was reaching its climax. His people were enjoying earthly prosperity in a material kingdom and were looking forward to expansion and further progress but they had other and more painful lessons to learn. All the majesty and pomp of their rulers, all the marble and gold of their capital, all their earthly prestige and power were but shadows of good things to come. This was the meaning of the exile. The temporal kingdom, of which they were so proud, was first divided, then destroyed. Assyrians crushed the Northern Kingdom where social injustice, lust for pleasure, unbridled vice, and cults of strange gods had long prevailed. Babylonians began the work of the purification of the Southern Kingdom by devastation, deportation, destruction of every trace of earthly greatness. The prophets had tried to prepare the people for the divine intervention; now they offered explanations of the heart-breaking catastrophes and repeated the promise of a new and eternal covenant, a new and eternal kingdom.

The return from exile marked the beginning of a period of waiting. Walls were rebuilt in Jerusalem, the law was re-established, the temple was restored. Men longed to hear the words "The kingdom of God is at hand!" They looked forward to seeing a messiah, sent by God and anointed by Him, who would preach the good tidings to the poor, who would bring comfort to the suffering, and open the eyes of the blind. Most of all, they scanned the words of the prophets, and waited to welcome one who would be their king.

Jesus came. They listened, hoped, wondered, and then

hardened their hearts when He began to teach that suffering is the way to glory. Only the pure of heart could see the beauty of His gospel. Only the meek understood that the land promised to Moses did not border on the Jordan. Only the poor in spirit knew what He meant when He told them about the Kingdom. Only the merciful understood the divine pity and the forgiveness that was theirs. Only the peacemakers knew what He wanted when He asked them to become like little children. Only those who mourned were comforted when He spoke. Only those who kept His laws and were persecuted for their fidelity had a place in His Kingdom. Only those who hungered and thirsted for the full observance of His laws found in the New Covenant the fulfillment of their heart's desires.

It was men blessed with these insights who would be His true witnesses throughout the world. Salvation had been accomplished in the fullness of time but salvation history would continue until the end of time. In it the world would appear as antagonist and as redeemed (to quote Jacques Maritain), to be finally condemned or to become part of the kingdom of God, triumphant and glorified. For in one sense this kingdom has come, in the form of the Church suffering and ever on pilgrimage; in another sense this kingdom is to come, in the form of the Church victorious and resting in the beauty of peace in the world beyond space and time.

Meanwhile men live in a world subject at every moment to two immanent movements which cross and contradict each other; one movement draws men upward toward the salvation for which they were made, the other movement draws men downward toward their destruction. Here and now the parable of the wheat and cockle explains men's danger and opportunity. It is the responsibility of Christians to further the growth of the good seed and draw all under the influence of the upward movement and to root out the weeds and weaken the power of the downward movement. They cannot escape from the law of the twofold contrasting progress but they can prepare for the eventual triumph of the Church, the coming of the new heaven and the new earth, which will be radiant, glorious, without spot or wrinkle, where death will be no more and God Himself will wipe away every tear.

Liturgical-Biblical-Catechetical Renewal

To live life in these perspectives is the great purpose of the liturgical, biblical, and catechetical renewal of our day as understood by the leaders of the Sister Formation Movement. This means praying in biblical concepts with the Church and for the great intentions of the Church. This means bringing the Paschal proclamation to all men. This means taking an active part in the history of salvation through the excellence of the spiritual, intellectual, and apostolic achievements of all religious women.

This movement is still in its early years. Much remains to be done. Its continuing success depends on many factors. One of these is a deepening understanding of lectio divina and the meaning of the history of salvation.

> These are only hints and guesses.
> Hints followed by guesses; and the rest
> Is prayer, observance, discipline, thought and action.

7

The People of God and Their Work

Edward J. Foye

A layman is a member of the People of God, of those who have been gathered together, assembled and formed by God. In this strict sense, "layman" is interchangeable with "Christian person," that is, all Christians—pope, cardinal, bishop, on down to the newly baptized infant—are laymen, members of the *laos Theou* (People of God). In the course of history, however, "laymen" came to mean those who have no especially defined function in the Church, if it may be so phrased. That is, laymen (*laikoi*) are those who are not called priests. However, the terms "layman" and "priest" represent an inadequate distinction, as the scholastics would say, between the ordained and the unordained: for, all priests are laymen and all laymen are priests. Terminological difficulties have been further compounded by the conflation of *sacerdos* and *presbyteros*. The word, "priest," is derived from *presbyteros* which means "elder," "one of the *digniores populi*." On the other hand, the word, "priest," is also used to translate *sacerdos* and *hiereus*. This ambiguity has led to an almost hopeless confusion of two distinct but not necessarily separate functions.

The *sacerdos* is the "holy-maker," the one who offers sacrifice for sins. In the New Covenant, there is but one high priest, Christ, who has entered *once and for all* into the Holy of Holies. All Christians, in virtue of baptism and the sealing of the Spirit, are "other Christs," who must decrease so that Christ might increase. All Christians are individual, and, therefore, imperfect, incarnations of Christ, being but His younger brothers. But when Christians come together in His name, they become Christ in a special way —He is in their midst. And it is He who offers the sacrifice; that is, Christ, incarnate in the Assembly of the People of God, renews and makes present His sacrifice through the communal activity.

Let us now turn to the presbyterial, or chirotonic (indicating the laying on of hands, ordination function. The *presbyteros*, or *chiroton*, participates in the episcopal office, that is, he, under the bishop, is a ruler, leader, shepherd, and overseer. The episcopacy's essential function is the overseeing of the order of the Work of the People of God, overseeing the activities of the Assembly, and passing judgment on the essential conformity of the doctrine proclaimed therein with the teaching that has been received from the apostles.

In this connection, it is important to note that *magister* is a translation of *episkopos*, and means at root, "superior," or "overseer," and not necessarily "teacher," although it seems to have very early taken on the meaning of "teacher" from the bishop's official supervisory connection with the teaching function in the Church. This teaching function like the prophetic, belongs to him to whom the Spirit, the Supreme Teacher in the Church, wills to give it directly. The supervisory, or episcopal, function, on the other hand, is conferred by the Spirit through the Church, and is therefore irrevocable—whence the indelibility of the sacramental character of orders, baptism, and confirmation; for when the Church binds, heaven binds. The *magisterium* approves or disapproves a teaching. It may at times give absolute approval to a teaching; that is, it may affirm that a particular teaching is a touchstone of true belief, as when it defines a dogma of the faith.

Thus the sacerdotal (or "sphragistic"), indicating the sealing of the Spirit, confirmation and the presbyterial are two distinct activities within the Church, and it is the latter and not the former that provides us with a basis for differentiating the ordained and the unordained.

The sacerdotal is participated in equally by all who have been Christened, that is, incorporated, inserted, into Christ. Thus the New Testament never employs *hiereus* or its equivalents of any but Christ and His Church: no New Testamentary individuals bear this dignity. Consequently, the distinction between the "general" and the "special" priesthood (*sacerdos-cum-presbyteros*) does not have its roots in the sacerdotal, but in the presbyterial. Is Christ divided? By no means!

Do the unordained participate in the presbyterial function? Only generally, and, in a special sense, reciprocally. For only someone who has been so ordered can preside at an Assembly of the People of God and intone the holy words of the anaphora. The "layman" for all of his priesthood, has not been so "ordered." He is a *sacerdos*, and he is so as much as any other person in the Church. As another Christ he is very definitely able to exercise his "holy-making" function in every aspect of his life. He is indeed a *sacerdos* forever, and this quality is present in everything he does.

Nevertheless, hands have not been laid upon him for an official, chirotonic, presbyterial, function in the Church. He has received the Spirit, but he has not received office.

As a consequence, the unordained may never preside at a public assembly; only one to whom the Assembly of the People of God has granted it may do so. The unordained may preside at a family meal, or, charismatically, at a private gathering. But, in order to preside at a public assembly, one must be a member of the official *presbyterium*.

Similarly, the unordained have a right to preach and teach in the Church, by virtue of having been sealed in the Spirit (according to Alcuin, confirmation is conferred *ad praedicandum aliis* = "to preach, to prophesy, to others"); but this charismatic "right" is always to be subject to those to whom it has been given to approve or disapprove in the Church.

Each member of the Church *is* the Church. Each member of the Church has authority (the ability to discern and proclaim the good) in the Church. This is because each completed member of the Church has been sealed in the Spirit. This authority pertains to the ordinary member of the Church charismatically, that is, by the gift of the Spirit. On the other hand, authority belongs officially, and sacramentally, to members of the *presbyterium*, and a fortiori, to the episcopacy. Thus it is in terms of the presbyterial that a distinction between "general" and "special" participation takes on relevancy: all Christians do share in the authority of Christ, but some do so charismatically, and others do so officially. It is in the hierarchical authority of the ordained that the Church specializes its authority.

Earlier the layman's reciprocal participation in the presbyterial function was mentioned: it might be expanded

upon. It is perhaps too seldom noted that the bishop is the
spouse of his diocese, the shepherd of his sheep, the leader
of his led, the ruler of his ruled. The generality enters into
the very definition of the bishop's speciality; and in this light
the master is truly the servant. Thus, for instance, ecclesial
teaching has always encouraged that a Mass be celebrated in
the presence of at least one other person, so that the action
may be that of the fullness of Christ—not that I would
imply that a solitary Mass is invalid. For, the Church (as
the communion of saints) supplies.

Throughout the foregoing, we have had to deal with an
odd terminology: *sacerdos* and *presbyteros*, sphragistic and
chirotonic, in order to make some distinctions. But this
terminology can be distracting; therefore, we will return to
a more ordinary vocabulary, using "priesthood" simply in
the sense of *sacerdotium*.

It was unfortunate, as it was historically inevitable, that
the distinction between the ordained and the unordained
came to be phrased in terms of a layman/priest dichotomy,
while the ancient and holy metaphor of shepherd and sheep
should remain relatively undeveloped. This false distinction between layman and priest has wrought great mischief
in our midst. We are just now beginning to understand the
nature of the Church and her worshiping activity, and
there are still many, many doctrinal problems yet to be
addressed and solved, but it is clear that through the impetus of the Spirit of Renewal in our midst that they will
be successfully handled in due time. But in the meantime
we are putting into practice the newly re-acquired appreciation of the priesthood of the Christian People through experiments with the participational or communitarian Mass.

This very fact will be a potent force for the easing of the tension that has come to be called lay-clerical, when the cleric and the ordinary Christian will have come, through the experience of their shared priesthood in the participational Mass, to a fuller appreciation of the depth and dignity of the Christian vocation itself, and will have shared the joy of loving Christ and one another in an experiential way, and will have received the peace which only Christ can give, and tension will have dissolved.

When I speak of participational Masses, I am not speaking of the simple dialogue or recited Mass, which makes altar boys of us all, and has the added disadvantage of giving undue emphasis to a part of the Mass that is really not a part of the Mass, the prayers at the foot of the altar. Nor do I mean the Gregorian Masses, because for all of their stateliness and loveliness, they suffer from the same lack of worthiness—shall we call it?—that dialogue Masses do: we are again reduced to being altar boys, hearing words we do not understand, saying things we cannot possibly mean from the depths of our souls. This, I would suggest, is a sorry condition for a royal priesthood to have to endure.

The ideal communitarian Mass would have all the parts proper to the Assembly said or sung by the Assembly in their ordinary tongue, and all the parts proper to the celebrant said or sung by the celebrant in that same tongue, and in the hearing of the Assembly so that it might give its assent.

This ideal Mass goes somewhat beyond what the schema of the Council proposes. We may very well be patient, for what has been granted goes well, well beyond the expectations of most men. Yet I have heard it said that much of the proposed changes are meant for the mission countries and that they would not be implemented in this country for ten or twenty years. I don't believe this; I believe that the leaders of our Church are much too far-sighted and pastoral-minded to overlook this one effective means for meeting the crisis in the American Church. But again I have heard it said that there is no crisis in the American Church. This statement I take to be the epitome of that crisis, which I would describe as one of place: among some there is a crisis of faith and they can no longer find place for a tyrannical Church in their lives; for others it is a frustrated love, they would like to be of the Church and not just in it, and they cannot find place. Therefore, it seems clear that if our Church is to be anything but a monument to lace-curtain respectability, it is imperative that the Church in the United States allow the liturgy to become a vital factor in the lives of its members. This means: as much of the Mass in English as is possible—and as soon as possible.

Through a Mass wherein all participants are able to consciously and properly exercise their priesthood, the Church will fill the lives of all Christians and they more-over will be more easily able to identify with the Church. Fully formed Christians will be incapable of criticizing the Church; they will and must scrutinize the Church, admit its shortcomings, just as they must with themselves. They will love the Church as they love themselves and their neighbor, for they will have identified with her.

Again, through participational Masses, Christians will be more readily able to perceive their vocations within the great Work of the People of God. To expatiate:

Since the priesthood of Christ is shared communally, it can only be really experienced communally, in the partici-pational Mass. Standing about the altar, Christians, in communion with Christ, with one another, with all Christians, with all men, with all creatures, offer praise and worship to the loving Godhead which has begotten us all: we give thanks for the being in which we move, the life by which we live, and the spirit by which we love. It can be a deeply moving experience. If the experience is emotional, the emotion is as yet unnamed; it is a combination of, at least, love, joy, and peace. It pervades, it abides, it is productive of deep interpersonal charity.

Before proceeding with a brief examination of the experience of community, let us advert to two dangers. One would be the superficiality that would begin to speak of "spiritual sweetness for the laity." This needs no more refutation than the knowledge that such statements are unhappily inevitable among human beings. The other danger is a fear of emotionalism among Catholics who rightly disapprove of finding themselves looking for statuary to start talking to them, or who feel that religious emotionalism must be frenzied, fanatic, or at least gauche. These doubts must be answered by a test of the spirit. The rule for this test is given a number of times in the New Testament. Or, one might rephrase the rule, using a psalm, "Taste and see . . ."

The experience of community has not been limited to participational Masses. It has also been reported in the *Cursillo* movement, although I have heard it said that the *Cursillo* experience does not abide. This may be expected, in that this marvelous retreat movement is not sacramental in essence. However, when the *Cursillo* is liturgically and participationally reinforced, as it is in some areas, grounds for this criticism seem to fall away.

The effect of the experience of community can be revolutionary. And it has, as I mentioned before, an abiding quality: it can change one's life. To put it in religious terms, the experience of community can induce a metanoia or conversion to a higher level of Christian life and awareness. This very fact has far-reaching ramifications in the realms of psychology and spirituality. We will not investigate the psychological off-shootings of the phenomenon, but will simply ask what the relationship is between maturity and Christian perfection in the light of the following:

The keynote of Christian spirituality has long been, "Be ye perfect as the heavenly Father is perfect." The heavenly Father is perfect in His Fatherhood—He is completely Father. The individual human being is made perfect by becoming this individual human being as intensely as can be: he becomes the personification of the values he holds dear. In other words, Christ could have said, "Become completely what you are," and would have meant almost the same thing. If you are completely what you are, you are without conflict, you are without guilt-feelings—and this is rather difficult for the individual human being to achieve. The only way a personality can become truly integrated is by one's values having been made one among themselves around a center. The center of values, or the bond of the virtues, is charity, which is God's very nature. To use Father Alfred Delp's saying, "God enters into the definition of man when man is fully man."

The law of man's specific nature is *recta ratio*, or, "Do the best you can according to your lights." The real law of nature, applicable to all of nature, is given in the Bible: "Increase and multiply." Our Creator has commanded us to intensify and proliferate. The boy Jesus intensified in wisdom. Intensification takes priority over proliferation; and thus men eat animals. (I believe that this law has application in the fertility-control controversy, but it should not detain us here.) Further it may be argued that Christ's injunction to perfection was not directed merely to outstanding members of the human race, but to all men, so that the human race as a whole may evolve into a higher form of being, to a higher level of God-consciousness.

Whether this evolution will be the occasion for the Second Coming of the Lord, or whether it will serve as a a further prelude thereto is an idle speculation. But it would seem to follow that the very process itself is communal and universal (hence the very deep relevance of *Pacem in terris*).

If the foregoing is true, as I believe it is, then the principal goal of the People of God is the fulfillment of the Will of God, the conversion of the whole of man and creation to the Spirit of God who moves all things; as brothers in charity we must urge each other on to perfection. To deny another Christian the right to full participation in the Mass is not simply to violate him in justice, in virtue of his priesthood; it is also to deny him an occasion for conversion, and it is therefore a sin against charity, the very nature of God.

It has been too seldom noted that the ergon element in the word, "liturgy," is etymologically related to an interesting group of words: work, urge, orgasm, orgy, erg, and more than likely Ur of the Chaldees. It is a growl, a groan, a spiration. It is a very basic human sound; it is a verbalized exhalation, a sigh.

That it should be the word used when speaking of the

activity of the Assembly indicates that the liturgy has a *mysterion* all its own. The liturgy recapitulates and symbolizes everything that man does. Man as priest dedicates in the liturgy all of his pseudo nonliturgical activity. But man as priest takes an atom and places it in the service of God's plan for salvation and intensification: thus it is no longer profane. He sends a rocket to the moon. He effects man's economic, therefore human, therefore salvific, progress. Man—Christian man, who has been initiated into the mysteries of the universe—is a priest every day of his life, every moment of his being.

It cannot be claimed that each Christian is conscious of, or acknowledges, his priesthood. Nor can it be claimed that each Christian recognizes the sacramental nature of his own contribution to human progress. Least of all can it be claimed that each Christian allows his priesthood to so pervade his life that he recognizes his right to preside over a familial sharing of bread and wine (or juice if necessary) before a meal using an invocation like this:

> Be in our midst, O Lord,
> And bless this bread and this loving cup,
> Which we share
> As a memorial of You
> As a sign of our love, of which You are the bond,
> And as a foretaste of Your coming, which we joyfully await.

8

The Parish: A Total View

JOSEPH M. CONNOLLY

In this country there have been many calls for bringing the renewal of the Church into the parish. Many important steps have been taken in this direction already. We have some parishes with a fine sense of the liturgy; some with a well-developed catechetical program; some which are working well in the social field, and some that are truly missionary in their convert activity. But it would seem that we are in need not of liturgical parishes, nor catechetical parishes nor missionary parishes, but rather of parishes which are directed by a total view, a view which starts from the very essence of the parish and embraces all of the areas that are proper to the parish.

Most of us are prevented from getting a total view, precisely because the totality of our own situations is so overpowering. Just to keep up with the day to day activities is enough to blind us to deeper considerations. As in so many other areas, poverty can perhaps give leisure and freedom so that one is able to take stock, plan an experiment, and try the experiment out. In this chapter I should like to re-

port on such a stocktaking and such an experiment. I am
emboldened thus to expose my own ignorance and failures,
not to crow, but rather to have the benefits of criticism, of
examination by disinterested observers, and in the hope
that perhaps others may be stimulated to do a bit of stocktaking and experimenting.

When I was invited to come to a crowded urban area,
encompassing 55,000 souls, but only 500 Catholics, I took
as my starting principle that the parish is the Church Universal, here and now. The concerns of the Universal Church
must be the concerns of this little local church. The major
thrusts and impulses of the Universal Church must find a
reverberation in this local church. To be in tune with these
concerns, thrusts, and impulses, I determined to bring to
bear on the parish problems the searching light of the
actions and teachings of the modern papacy, and more recently the actions of the Council.

In summary form I think that the modern papacy has
operated in the following manner: to make a rediscovery of
the nature of the Church as more than a juridical reality,
and in the light of this new vision of the Church to look at
the way the Church worships, to look at the way in which
she forms Christ in men, to look not only at the way she
brings the Gospel to the city of men, but also at the way
in which she puts that Gospel and its grace at the service of
the men of the city by social action.

Another summation could envision the Church, aware of
her full dignity and dimensions, looking inwardly upon herself; looking at her worship, her teaching, her distributing
of roles among her members; and then looking outwardly
at those who have not been evangelized, at those who are
not of her unity, and at the whole realm of man's social life.

In the neo-scholastic jargon of the last decade, this is an ensemble of Liturgical–Catechetical–Missionary–Ecumenical–Lay Apostle–Social Action apostolate which flows from an ever-richer ecclesiology.

Let us try to see how this works out in reality. If we really admit that the Church is the Mystical Body of Christ, then the parish is an organ of this Body. If the Church is the Mystic Vine of which Christ is the stock and men are the branches, then the parish is a cluster of branches. If the Church is the Kingdom, then the parish is a province. If the Church is a temple made of living stones, then the parish is a set of rooms in the temple. If the Church is Christ teaching men today, saving men today, making men holy today, then the parish must be teaching, saving, and making men holy. If the Church is Christ stretched across time and space, then the parish must be Christ here and now, in this territory, for these people. These biblical definitions of the church are not illusions, they are not haunting dreams calling us back to some romantic past or luring us to some unforseen future. The Church is a living pulsating thing, but it exists here and now on the local level in the parish.

Of course the parish is not the Church Universal, it is a part, and as a part it can make demands on the whole and can make contributions to the whole. But within this limitation the parish must realize that it is the Church. The parish is *this* portion of the flock of the Lord, it is *this* gathering of people worshiping the Father in spirit and in truth, raising up new sons and daughters to God, making up what is lacking in the sufferings of Christ, carrying the daily message of the love of God in Christ to its city, going up finally in the Body of the Resurrection.

In such a vision one would hope that it would be impossible for an overanxious administrator to make the statement that the parish exists for the school.

Certainly, if we are to become aware that the parish is the Mystical Body here, as *this* portion of the People of God, we cannot do this by talking about it, we must have an experience of it. Until it is experienced, community, like love, is unknown, it is not something that can be vicariously shared, or lectured about. The normal way for the Christian to have an experience of community is by worship.

Only when the Christian experiences that his coming to church is in response to God's call; that he is with his brothers, grouped around the altar performing a symphonic function, perfectly willing to perform his prayers and songs and also to attend to the actions of others, willing to listen and to see, and in listening to receive; only when he experiences himself one with the other members of the community, and through them one with Christ, only when this happens, not rarely but regularly, will he be able to sense himself and his parish as they are in the mind of God. This is the only reason for the reform of the liturgy: to make the Mass, Sunday for all, daily for some, a living experience of being the Church, of being one with his brothers, one with his elder Brother Jesus, in a shared experience of receiving from God with each other, of giving to God with each other.

The Fathers of the Second Vatican Council have pointed out that the parish worship is the direct mirror of that unique worship which is performed by the bishop, surrounded by his priest, his ministers, and his people. The very fact of the size of the Church today makes this communion with one's bishop impossible. It is in the parish church that the local family worship is capable of coming into reality. The purpose of the conciliar reform is to so open the form of the Mass that the parish experience can be real for all parishioners and all parishes.

When one has had this experience, and like the crowds of old can glorify God for "the wonders we have seen," there is only one thing that he can do, share what he has received. He wants to share these things more deeply with those of the household of the Faith and those outside; he wants to share them with his children and with the other adults of the parish; he wants to carry them as lights to those who sit in darkness, to take their fullness to those who have only a diminished portion. He wants to set them loose in his city.

The missionary impulse of the parish is twofold: to further perfect and form the already Catholic, and to bring the fullness of the Faith to the non-Catholic.

The normal attitude to formation and education of the already Catholic has been foreshortened by the tremendous effort made to create and maintain our school system. But this foreshortening has limited our attention to the child, the adult we have left to his own devices. But here again a restored liturgy will step in and once again do a job which it was meant to do. For the liturgy, by using the symbolic imaginative language of Scripture, by speaking directly to the whole man by signs, is an educating, formation-giving process that is operative in all people at all stages of their lives.

But the times in which we live, times in which the man who is a member of the parish is also an adult, mature citizen who hires his governors, who votes on the general

plan for state and country, these times call forth from the
Church and thus from the parish an effort to include the
lay adult member in the functioning and operation of the
parish. Men as ministers at the altar (instead of relegating
serving to tiny tots), men as lector-commentators and as
cantors at Mass, men and women as teachers, principals
and assistants in the CCD school of religion, men and
women doing the clerical work: these positions of lay ad-
ministration are found in many parishes. But more is
needed. The parish should consider itself as a natural place
in which all of the talents of all of the people are utilized,
with due respect for their competence, and their freedom.
This time of transition, when we are leaving the era of the
King-Father, child-subject relationship and are moving into
the mutually trusting adult-to-adult relationship will demand a great deal of charity, of frankness, and of suffering
on the part of all. To encourage my priest readers, may I
hold out to them the hope that, as the loss of the Papal
States liberated the papacy and made it much more effective as a spiritual and moral leader, so the liberation of the
pastor and his curates from the omnicompetence they have
striven for in the past should enhance their truly priestly
position. And for the encouragement of my lay readers, may
I suggest that those who are closer to the problems of
growth should strive for that patience which the young
do not have by nature.

If there is any area of parish life that needs to be completely re-examined, it is the process by which we take in-
quirers and form them into catechumens, and lead them to
baptism. As part of this re-examination I should like to
share with you the experiments we have made. Recall
to mind my opening statement that this sharing is done

merely to trigger a sharp criticism and to spur others to experiment in their own area.

The common practice in this country is based on the desire for a rapid formation, completed in a matter of months. Underlying this decision for speed is an assumption that only a priest can be a catechist for adult converts. Since there are so few priests available, it was considered necessary to limit the time of the instruction period, so as to spread the priest around. Perhaps if we by-passed the question of who the teachers will be and look at the needs of the pupil, we would come to another answer to the question of how long the instructions should last.

We have sought to imitate nature and recognize the fact that the passage of time is an integral element in the process of growth. From conception to birth, from infancy to adolescence to maturity; all of this requires time. The same is true in the process of growth in knowledge. If all we want to do is to implant ideas and concepts, to stock a well-developed memory with data, then we can afford a short cut. But when we want the knower to become what he knows, when we want the knowledge to become motive for action, when we want to influence the whole man, not merely from the ears up, but also from the ears down; when we want to transmute knowledge into wisdom and life, time is a factor which cannot be minimized. We have chosen to lengthen our catechumen's instructions to eighteen months.

Before a catechumen can become a member of the Church he must first become a member of the parish community. The conditions of membership in the parish community can be less rigorous, even provisional, than those for membership in the Church as such. All it takes is the expressed desire to study the Church. This desire is then formalized by a mutual exchange of pledges: the catechumen pledges himself to be faithful to weekly Mass and class, until called to Baptism, and the parish pledges him the best instructions the parish can provide, and his freedom to withdraw from the catechumenate if his conscience so dictates. This mutual pledging is done before the whole parish community, is followed by prayers by the pastor, and is sealed by the transmission of a token of induction. Thus the catechumen is a part of the parish. Of course his catechist is also a member of the parish, as are the people who brought him thus far and those who will support him as he grows in the knowledge of the faith. Thus received, the catechumen is not then forgotten by the parish community. Periodically, every three months, he is publicly promoted, and the pledges are renewed. Thus the community sees the catechumen advance, patiently, through the stages of the catechumenate.

If one is realistic and looks at eighteen months, one sees that the catechumen may get weary, and need to be prodded; may get discouraged, and need a shoulder to cry on; may have moments of joy and want to share them with a personal friend who can understand his joy; so the parish assigns a shepherd to each catechumen, a shepherd who will shoulder the journeying lamb.

Within the parish catechumenate, the formation of the catechumen comes primarily from the Mass. This is the real school of the disciples of the Lord. And this is a pressing reason for the average American parish to adopt the restored liturgy as soon as possible. But in addition there are the regular classes of instruction for the catechumens. A sharp-eyed examination of the methods and content of the catechesis of converts is being done throughout the country, but it needs to be furthered and expanded. At this point I should like merely to raise the question of having other than priest catechists employed in this work. Long experience has shown us that nuns and lay people can pass the mystery on to our children in the parochial school and in the CCD. This experience should lead one to the conclusion that what can be done for children can be done for adults as well. Certainly the CCD will have to develop more thorough training courses for such lay catechists. Certainly the spiritual formation to be given them must be more mature. But who would dare to say that the CCD cannot develop these courses, or that the American priest cannot give this direction to his parish catechists? I make this plea for the development of lay catechists because I am faced, in microcosm, with the basic problem that is blocking the conversion of America. Our parish has 55,000 souls. If all possible converts are to be trained by only the two priests of the parish, we must necessarily lower our hopes before this group of 55,000. The larger problem of the whole country merely shows the problem on a larger scale. Subtract the number of Catholics from the number of Americans and divide the difference by the number of priests and you will see what I mean.

When the parish looks outside its own membership it finds not only the great masses of the unchurched, it also finds that large number of sincere Protestants who make up the congregations of the neighboring churches—men and women whose vocation has cast them as committed Christians with a denominational allegiance, who are hearing God's word and are receiving God's graces through these bodies. Thus the parish is confronted with the whole ecumenical problem. Because we in America are so new at the ecumenical work, and because our Catholic brothers in Europe have done little on a grass-roots level, we have practically no source of guidance that can be given generally, except, of course, the need to alert our people to the scandal that is division and to the hopes and desires for unity that the Holy Spirit has stirred up within and without the Church. The parish prayer-life can be directed to a spirit of contrition on the part of Catholics for our share in the schisms, and to a spirit of faithful entreaty that the day may be hastened when the prayer of the Lord may be fulfilled, that there may be "one flock and one shepherd."

While our Catholic experience is limited, we can profit from the advice that our separated brothers can give us from their almost fifty years of effort. Dr. Eugene Carson Blake has outlined four stages that individuals and denominations go through as they engage in ecumenical efforts. First there is joy: joy that one can be with his brother; joy in the discovery that in spite of differences there is still much that we share. Then there is a discovery of how little I know about my own tradition and the positions of my own Church, and this leads to a deeper study of what I am myself, so that I can bear better witness to the truth that has been given me. As the work progresses, the meager results lead to a temptation to despair that anything concrete can happen; frustration destroys the early hopes, precisely because these early hopes were pinned to human effort. If one is able to avoid the temptation to quit at this stage, one is finally led to a more pure faith in the workings of the Holy Spirit, a more confident reliance on the will and the methods of Our Father, a more conscious dependence upon Christ and His power, rather than on the craftiness of men.

These stages: Joy, *ressourcement*, frustration, and finally faith; have been experienced time and again by persons of all groups and by many groups. As our American parishes try to place themselves at the service of the Spirit in trying to heal breaches of long standing, they will have to go through these four stages.

In facing the social problems of the area which makes up the parish, one can also envision a spirit of brotherly cooperation with the local Protestant churches. A unity of faith is not needed to give a common service of justice and charity.

This reference to the possibility of cooperation with the Protestants in the work of helping in civic problems leads us to the further response of the parish when it realizes that the parish is Christ here with His wisdom, His demands of justice, His helpful charity and grace.

The parish is in the city of men. While it must call men to the city of God, it is nonetheless an institution among institutions. It owns property, it uses public utilities, it helps to lift up or to tear down its own neighborhood. But much more than this the parish has a prophetic and a ministering function to perform. Its prophecy is exercised when it raises up articulate, animated men and women who will be in the forefront of the planning for the city that is constantly being reborn. Men and women who will take the time to learn all of the grubby details that must go into master planning, and yet who will not let the human, personal aspects of the city be submerged by the political, economic, or bricks-and-mortar components.

The parish's ministering function may strike some people
as novel, because it is novel. The classical understanding of
the works of mercy was limited to the wiping of individual
noses and the changing of individual diapers. But with the
vast throngs of people who make up the modern urban
complex, this individual approach is out-dated. Govern-
ment has had to enter the picture and Public Welfare is
properly involved in most areas which were previously the
exclusive domain of the Church. And yet the very size of
the Welfare operation creates little nooks and crannies in
which individuals can get lost. For instance, when a client
goes to welfare, he may be told to come back in two weeks,
but they do not put the man or his family in deep freeze
for these two weeks. There must be somewhere that this
man, a human person, can go to receive the food and rent
and help that he needs until the mammoth Public Welfare
can shift its gears for him. Naturally this is the parish.
The parish must assume this role of wiping individual
noses. The novelty of this situation comes in when we
realize that by filling in for the finer details for Public Welfare, we are constantly in danger of working only with
the "undeserving" poor. Men and women who do not fit
on an IBM card, cases that are so odd that they have not yet
been classified, these are the little ones that Christ in His
parish church must have compassion on and must minister
to. In the face of the smug middle-class carefulness of much
that passes for Catholic charities in this country, I for one
rejoice that we are forced back to the least of His brethren.

If, through its worship and the workings of its inner life,
the parish really has become a community, it will have produced people who know what a community is and what it

can do. They will then be able to go out to their neighbor-
hoods and help to create communities there.

If, through its preaching and example, the parish makes
its people aware of the demands of social justice as trum-
peted by the modern popes, it will send its people into the
forefront of all battles for justice and for peace.

In the preamble to the Sermon on the Mount, Jesus
gave His blessing to peacemakers, searchers for justice, and
merciful men. And yet where are these men blessed by Jesus
in our present-day America? The secularist and the Quaker
are in the positions of leadership and of witness, the Protestant and the Jew are right beside them. Where are the
Catholics? *Pacem in terris* came as a rude shock to many
Catholics; yet with the possible exception of the over-
tures of conversations with the Communists, it added very
little to the massive works of Pius XII on the question of
peace. American Catholic cooperation in peace efforts can
be measured by the milimeters, while our antismut cam-
paigns stretch out for kilometers.

World peace may seem quite remote from a parish, and
yet there is in every American city an area of almost de-
clared warfare which cries out for peacemakers, and which
confronts every urban parishioner. That is the race question.
No matter how lily-white the parish may be, its parishioners
are never far from some Negroes. No matter how far their
flight may have taken them from the black ghettoes, they
still go into the city, they still meet their fellow white man,
they still work near some colored brother. If there is to be a
significant Catholic contribution to the cause of racial
justice and peace, it can be made only when every parish,
and therefore every parishioner, has examined his thinking,

attitudes, and conduct in the light of the teachings of our faith about the unity of the human family, the demands of social justice, and the urgings of charity. This examination will be hard to do, but if it is done as a part of a parish effort, it will be made with the mutual support of brothers, under the experienced sign of brotherhood which is the restored liturgy.

In summary, it can be said that when the parish is what it should be, it will not only raise up sons and daughters of God, but it will also produce men and women for the city of man, who will bring to that city the powers of Christ and His love. The city of man, as long as it is merely a society, can call upon justice alone to be its binding force. Only when a non civil power provides it with an abundance of charity can it be transformed into a community. This transfusion of charity is the unique contribution of the citizens of the Kingdom of God who pass their pilgrimage here in the city of man. The state as such cannot demand this of us, but the state of our brothers in their misery, even in plenty, certainly calls out to us with a cry which should pierce our hearts.

A total view of the parish tries to see the parish as the Church in miniature: conscious of itself as Christ here and now, teaching, saving, and making men holy in this limited territory; in and through and with Christ worshipping the Father in the Spirit; forming Christ in his flock, reaching out to the other sheep, in isolation or in other flocks; ministering to the sick, the poor, and the needy in the world, and helping to perfect the city of man. This is a view, or a vision, which brings a balance to our appraisals, energy to our work, and warmth to our hearts as we try to become what we are, the People of God here and now.

9

Liturgy and the Social Order

ROBERT G. HOYT

I am not a specialist on the liturgy, nor on social justice; what I have to say about the relation between liturgy and social order has to come for the most part from my experience as a diocesan newspaper editor. It happens that in the week I began thinking about this piece we published a lengthy and sympathetic interview with a Negro Methodist minister, a disciple of Martin Luther King, about the techniques, goals and inner meaning of nonviolent direct action for civil rights. On the day of publication a subscriber called to protest against the appearance of such material in a Catholic paper. She conceded that there might be a few Catholic Negroes who were "all right"—presumably bleached by baptism; but an interview with a Protestant Negro! What was of interest in her call, however, was not her prejudice but her puzzlement; what did "all that sort of thing" have to do with *religion?*

Another telephone call the following week presented a somewhat more subtle problem. That week a committee of the state legislature had killed a bill to provide bus transportation to children attending parochial schools. My caller was angry not only at the legislators on the committee but also at the bishop and the diocesan paper; they had not done enough to push the school bus bill, but they were always making "phony statements" about the rights of "the niggers." On questioning, my caller did not deny that Negroes as a group suffer rather more serious disadvantages than do Catholics as a group; but this did not affect his argument, for his premise was that Catholics, and especially their leaders and their publications, should measure the importance of issues by their effect on the fortunes of individual Catholics and of the Church. What the bishop and the paper had forgotten was a great and central truth, that charity begins at home.

These incidents occurred shortly after Easter. In the previous Holy Week, our issue published on Good Friday carried a photographic interpretation of the Stations of the Cross, based on the scriptural meditation on the Way of the Cross contained in Helicon's *Layman's Missal*. The photos selected by managing editor Michael Greene were very far from being literal. The one for the fourteenth station, Jesus' Body Is Laid in the Tomb, was full of happy faces—priest, sponsors, parents smiling down at an infant about to be baptized. The scriptural passage was taken from the Epistle to the Romans: "And you, too, must think of yourselves as dead to sin, and alive with a life that looks toward God, through Christ Jesus our Lord."

For the first station, Jesus Is Condemned to Death, the quotation was from St. John's Gospel (11:52): "And not only for that nation's sake, but so as to bring together into one all God's children, scattered far and wide"; and the photograph showed a missionary nun distributing food to eager Korean children. I personally was most struck by the picture used in connection with the eleventh station, Jesus Is Nailed to the Cross; it showed simply a bare and desolate rural landscape overhung by lowering clouds; a railway crossing sign stood in the foreground, and telephone poles in the middle and far distance.

Other photographs showed a prisoner looking out through bars, a little boy helping his mother with dishes, an old man laboriously climbing institutional stairs toward his institutional room, a young woman at prayer, a hand-clasp. What the pictures showed, I think, was the universal relevancy of Christ; or, taking it the other way around, the ability of the mind, when it has been taught and invited to reflect, to seize on any slice of reality and find hints, symbols, reminders of Christ. But we got complaints that the presentation had made the Stations of the Cross too "ordinary," had destroyed the sacredness of these sacred events and eliminated the sense of tragedy from them.

The point of the first two incidents is evident enough, so it can be developed at leisure. It will not be so immediately clear why the third is included. Its relevance is that religion is always in danger of becoming a specialized source of a specialized kind of experience. Religious people are people who talk piously and with unction about religious matters; and a lovers' handclasp, a child trying on a new dress, a boy washing dishes, a prisoner under the weight of his guilt—these are not part of religion. When you "make" the stations, you are to concentrate on the physical suffering of the Saviour and on your sins which caused it; to encourage a free flow of images is not a proper piety.

The moral is really the same in the other incidents. The

woman who could see no connection between religion and race has succeeded at least partially in redefining religion so that it does not touch her inner moral attitudes. (She was very sure of her definition—Pope John's views on racism were simply Pope John's views.) And the man who was angry about the order of priorities evident in the policy of his bishop and his Catholic paper made manifest that for him the Church—at least in its relationship to the general community—is essentially an organized minority with the same license to pursue its own interests as any other pressure group.

I do not venture to say that such narrowness of understanding is typical, but certainly it is not rare. In the matter of race, for example, any Catholic of my generation—lay or clerical—could easily have reached maturity with an undisturbed racist conscience. My own diocese recently observed an Interracial Justice Week; for many Catholics it marked the first occasion that the subject of race had been mentioned from the pulpit. (In many other dioceses, of course, the occasion is still in the future.) One priest, a man of great good will and pastoral concern, and incidentally a man deeply in sympathy with the liturgical movement, found it necessary to observe that since the subject was so "touchy" and he was inexpert on it, he would follow exactly the sermon outline sent from the chancery. Yet racial injustice is the most obvious, most serious, best documented social evil of the times; what is to be thought of a religious teacher who cannot speak to his people about it of his own knowledge, out of his own heart?

As for the pressure-group mentality, it is perhaps most clearly operative in the selection of areas of Catholic concern. Responding to the emphasis on freedom in Pope John XXIII's encyclical *Pacem in terris*, columnist Norma Herzfeld asserted that American Catholics have been inclined to show a special interest in freedom only where the freedom of Catholics was in question. Meantime we have been inclined to condone or at least to blink at other varieties of persecution, especially the types carried out in the name of anticommunism. "Thus we are likely to hold public prayers for our persecuted brethren behind the Iron Curtain, but not for the persecuted black men of South Africa or our own persecuted fellow citizens in the slums downtown."

At a still deeper level the message of *Pacem in terris* was still more perplexing to many Catholics. In one of the earliest commentaries on the encyclical, Fr. Edward Duff, S.J., was moved to remark that its supranational perspective and its positive orientation would find the American Catholic community not well prepared to respond. Anticommunism has served all too many of us as an all-sufficient guide for thinking about world affairs; the polarization of the world between communist and "noncommunist" nations was the supreme political reality. Thus it came as something of a shock to find, not the defeat of communism, but the international political common good proposed by Pope John as the goal of policy. This struck even some of the friendliest commentators as utopian—noble and beautiful of course, but perhaps the least bit woolly-headed. The pursuit of the common good of the world community is a very Catholic idea; and a great novelty among American Catholics.

What has all this to do with liturgy? The answer comes easily, perhaps too easily, from liturgical enthusiasts.

The liturgy is the Mystical Body at prayer, Christ and His members united in worship of the Father, and thereby united in love with one another. The unity wrought by the liturgy is real on several levels. It unites them physically, simply because to celebrate it men gather in a given place and join their voices and coordinate their movements as the ritual directs. It effects a spiritual (intellectual, volitional, emotional) unity because it focuses the minds of the worshipers in common on the central Christian realities and seeks to elicit from all, in degrees corresponding to the capacity of each, the same interior acts of adoration and love. Most significantly, the liturgy unites men sacramentally; eating the same Bread, they live the same life. This reaches beyond physical intimacy and moral-intellectual unity to a level of actuality we can but dimly conceive, so that we express it only in metaphor: we are branches of one Vine, stones of a living Temple, members of one Body.

Says the liturgist: For all these reasons and on all these levels, the liturgy is the instrument best adapted to form in those who celebrate it a distinctively Christian social consciousness. Nobody pretends that the process is automatic. The liturgy can be celebrated in such a way that the crowd at Mass is nothing more than a crowd, at least in the consciousness of its members. It can be explained, and sometimes still is explained, in a fashion that will not upset the most individualistic conceptions of worship and of salvation. But the liturgy understood according to its true nature does have as its purpose (its teaching purpose and its substantive purpose) what Cecily Hastings has described as the "point" of Catholicism: The union of men with God in Christ. We pray and sing together because, being many, we are one—and in order to be one. The unity we glimpse in the liturgy is the oneness intended by God for His People; we do not submerge ourselves in a collectivity, but freely and humanly join our incompleteness with the insufficiency of others to form a community of worship. Freely and humanly: this community is formed by choice, not by accidental happenstance, and this choice is based not on shared emotion or "psychic contagion" but ideally on the insight each member is given into the truth the liturgy teaches, that we were not made by God or redeemed by Christ as so many monads but as members of one family, cells of one Body. The truth is communicated, of course, not as a political principle or sociological finding, but as an element of sacred history, a truth of faith; but this is not to say that it is a truth without application outside the walls of the parish church. Sacred history is simply a category of reality; what we learn from it is simply our true situation.

These reflections have been put forward as a sort of gloss on the famous dictum that the liturgy is the "primary and indispensable source of the true Christian spirit." This is the answer very properly offered when query is made of the connection between the liturgy and social justice. I have suggested, however, that the answer comes too easily from liturgical enthusiasts, and I wanted to make clear that I understood something of what the answer is before entering my criticism.

The criticism itself is simple enough. The liturgy is indeed the primary and indispensable source of Christian formation, but it is not the only or the sufficient source; and this is something liturgists, especially in these latter days, need to reflect upon. Despite all the ties of sympathy

and mutual respect between the liturgical and social movements, I think it is simply a fact that the former has not
yet given the latter the support it needs. Liturgists have not
understood to what extent the translation of liturgical piety
into concern for the multitude is a test of the truth and
depth of their spirituality.

These are bald and perhaps crude assertions; I can not
document but only illustrate them. A passage from the
diary kept by Fr. Alfred Delp, S.J., in the days before his
execution by the Nazis will serve as a starter. Reflecting on
the Church's loss of influence over the affairs of the world,
he wrote:

"The Church faces the same tasks that nations and
states and the western world in general have to face—the
problem of man, how he is to be housed and fed and how
he can be employed in order to support himself. In other
words we need social and economic regeneration. And then
man also must be made aware of his true nature—in
other words we need intellectual and religious regeneration.
These are problems for the world, for individual states and
nations, and they are also problems for the Church—far
more so, for instance, than the question of liturgical forms.
If these problems are solved without us, or to our disadvantage, then the whole of Europe will be lost to the Church,
even if every altar faces the people and Gregorian chant is
the rule of every parish."

There is a distinction—invented for the purpose of this
essay—between professional religionists and religious professionals. Neither term is particularly savory, but in the
present order of things there have to be religious professionals, clerics or laymen whose work it is to administer
the affairs of religion. This work includes the task of ex-

pounding the truths of religion. Religious professionals become professional religionists when they begin to refine and manipulate concepts without reference to their own experience or the needs and experiences of those to whom they minister. This seems to be the phenomenon Thomas Merton refers to in his introduction to the published version of Father Delp's prison writings[1] when he speaks of the "much publicized movements" within the Church which, "seen from the silence of Father Delp's prison cell . . . take on a pitiable air of insignificance." And he adds: "Instead of being aimed at those whom the Church most needs to seek, these movements seem to him [Father Delp] in many cases to concern themselves with the hunger of pious souls for their own satisfaction: they produce an illusion of holiness and a gratifying sense that one is accomplishing something." Is Father Merton talking about the liturgical movement? I do not know; but I have heard many a sermon on the Mystical Body or on the liturgy made by preachers who did not know what the lives of their hearers were like. These sermons are lofty indeed; they are spoken from the clouds rather than merely from the mountaintop. And in liturgical journals I do not see that a great deal is being done to bring these preachers back to earth.

The quotation from Father Delp may suggest that to his mind (and mine), solving the housing problem has priority over the renewal and right ordering of Catholic worship. No; but the connection between these tasks must be seen. It is not a relationship of means to ends; we do not teach the social dimension of worship in order to bring about a commitment to social justice. But if increased social awareness and compassion do not follow from liturgical renewal, there is reason to question the realism of the movement. I have no wish to make the preacher a moralizer or a social analyst, a solver of the world's complex problems; but I have sometimes thought that when we invited our children to add an extra Hail Mary to their night prayers on behalf of the people of Algeria or the Congo or Little Rock, we conveyed an idea they had not been offered elsewhere.

In his 1960 Cardinal Bellarmine Lecture at St. Mary's College, Fr. Godfrey Diekmann, O.S.B., remarked that in his many travels he has heard many comments about the peculiarities proper to Catholics, but never a suggestion—"not even the beginning of a hint!"—that Catholics are different because they have greater love for one another. "We have the sacrament of fellowship, the sacrament which gives us the grace of fellowship and really unites us. The gift, therefore, becomes our obligation. If it does not make an impact on American life, is it perhaps because we ourselves have never understood this element of the Eucharist adequately? Have we never taught our people that kneeling together means opening our hearts to each other? Otherwise we are not receiving Christ worthily."

Among the evils now present in the world none are more powerful or pervasive than nationalism and racism. I know of no evidence to suggest that Catholics as a group are less affected by these attitudes than are other groups. Sociologically speaking, one does not think of a Catholic as one who is more likely than the next man to be integrationist or internationalist in his outlook. Nationalism and racism are spiritual rather than political evils at root; they rise out of attitudes radically opposed to Christianity. At the moment racism is the more immediately obvious and the

more obviously ugly of the two; but in the end nationalism
may be charged with a greater potential of catastrophe. Can
it be said that these evils are better understood and resisted
in the average "liturgical parish" than elsewhere? Upon reflection I think the answer is probably "Yes, but . . ."
The pastor interested in the aims of the liturgical movement is quite likely to be interested also in social reform
and to follow papal leadership on the world order as on the
mode of worship, and to be aware of the relationship between the two. On the other hand, I do not believe the
liturgical movement itself has encouraged this pastor to
teach this relationship, to see its communication as all-
important, deserving his highest ingenuity and most devoted effort. The references are there, but they are occasional and peripheral when they should be central and
frequent.

It may be said that these criticisms if accepted might
destroy the special characteristics of the liturgical movement,
cause it to lose sight of its specific objectives and to assume
burdens properly belonging to other movements in the
Church; *Worship* (for example) would try to take over the
responsibilities of *Social Order* and in doing so no longer
contribute to the deepening of liturgical scholarship. Having no reputation as a scholar or religious thinker to lose, I
have the temerity to suggest that perhaps these risks need
to be taken. The reason is not that the race question and
the peace issue and the problem of labor-management relations are so pressing that they need a greater share
of our attention for a while; it is rather that our
religion-in-practice lacks a dimension proper to it, which
I have been calling social awareness, and the liturgy is not
now being made to serve the people as a primary source of

that awareness. It really ought not to be possible for the liturgical movement to flourish as it has flourished without creating any notable concern about the arms race, the absence of a world order, the disparity in wealth and hope between the rich nations and the poor nations, and about interracial, interreligious and intercultural hostilities—to list only a few of the "problems" the Christian encounters in the world, toward which he must assume an attitude, for whose solution he is responsible in some measure.

When the case is put as it has been here, there is a temptation perhaps to dismiss it as a delayed echo of the enthusiasm of earlier times for the "social gospel" and to suspect that the writer is unaware of recent developments in scriptural studies, in moral theology, and in catechetics, and of the potential influence of these developments in fostering a free, personal, mature Christian response to the challenges of the time. I do not wish to minimize the significance of these insights, nor to exaggerate my own slight grasp of them; but for the sake of discussion I will file a countercharge. As a layman with a certain bias toward the social apostolate I find in much discussion of these themes a tendency toward enthusiasm for new vocabulary, a tendency to juggle concepts and a tendency to keep religion a thing apart from what is going on in the world. Here again is Father Merton, interpreting Father Delp: "Too much religious action today . . . concentrates on the relatively minor problems of the religious-minded minority and ignores the great issues which compromise the very survival of the human race."

The social gospel was a shallow and merely moralistic version of Christianity. The difference between it and the social doctrine of the Church is not adequately suggested when one speaks only in terms of "social awareness" or even of "social justice." The social thought of Christians (and not only of Christians) is moving at many levels and from many perspectives toward preoccupation with the unity of mankind and the inviolability of the human person. One thinks of Pope John's acceptance of the concepts of world justice in *Mater et Magistra* and of world community in *Pacem in terris;* of his rejection of racism, of ideological crusading, of absolute national sovereignty. The ecumenical movement in all its forms reflects the same preoccupation, and the thought of Pierre Teilhard de Chardin represents an ambitious and significant attempt to interpret the whole of cosmic history as oriented toward achievement of a unity not yet conceivable.

This new emphasis does not cancel out previous formulations of the Catholic's obligations in justice and charity toward the social order. But it seems to find the root evil of injustice and of the withholding of love in their divisiveness, which stands in the way blocking fulfillment of God's plan for the family of man. Surely this tendency is in perfect harmony with the genius of the liturgical movement; surely both movements can gain by borrowing more freely from each other.

NOTE

[1] *The Prison Meditations of Father Alfred Delp* (New York: Herder and Herder, 1963).

10

Religious Art and Architecture Today

MAURICE LAVANOUX

It has become increasingly evident that any discussion of religious art and architecture assumes a definite approach to the question of art itself and to the design of our churches today. Up to the period following the First World War and well into the 1930s the approach to religious art and architecture was largely negative and conditioned by nostalgia for the past. It was then the heyday of the pseudo-Gothic, pseudo-Romanesque revival, of which the results can be seen in many cities and on many a university campus. This nostalgic tendency represented what can be called the straitjacket approach, in which a preconceived style was deliberately used even in defiance of changing conditions. However, the definite, dynamic approach to church architecture, which is at the core of any sensible solution that a talented architect today would propose, is conditioned by the primacy of the liturgy. For when we speak of religious art—that is, art at the service of the Church—we must place first things first and reason from the point of view of the liturgy. We know that the liturgy is the Church's public and lawful act of worship. Insofar as the artist and architect are concerned this liturgy can be taken to mean a climate, an atmosphere, informed by the fact that it is the official worship of the Church. Thus, if artists and architects, and their clients as well, take the liturgy seriously, the design and plan of new churches will be based on the liturgy. That is, art will be determined by its relation to, and in the service of, that liturgy. In this sense, the well-known formula, "form follows function," takes on a new significance.

This relation of art to the liturgy was well brought out by the noted theologian, Romano Guardini:

The Church has not built up the *Opus Dei* for the pleasure of forming beautiful symbols, choice language, and graceful, stately gestures. She has done it—insofar as it is not completely devoted to the worship of God—for the sake of our desperate spiritual need. It is to give expression to the events of the Christian's inner life: the assimilation, through the Holy Ghost, of the life of the creature to the life of God in Christ; the actual and genuine rebirth of the creature into a new existence. . . . All this in the continued mystic renewal of Christ's life in the course of the ecclesiastical year. The fulfillment of all these processes by the set form of language, gesture, and instruments, their revelation, teaching, accomplishment and acceptance by the faithful, together constitute the liturgy. We see, then, that it is primarily concerned with reality, with the approach of the real creature to a real God, and with the profoundly real and serious matter of the redemption. *There is here no question of creating beauty,* but of finding salvation for sin-stricken humanity. *Here truth is at stake,* and the fate of the soul, and real—yes, ultimately the only real—life. All this it is which must be revealed, expressed, sought after, found, and imparted by every possible means and method; and when this is accomplished, lo! *it is turned into beauty.*[1]

We see, then, that the spiritual quality, of what we can call the emotional impact of the liturgy, should surely result in art. It is this atmosphere, this climate, this frame of mind that is important. In a way these are the intangibles of any problem of architectural design but they are crucial intangibles that can help and inspire the architect and artist to overcome the sterility that engulfs so much work today.

Incidentally, if we do take these matters seriously, and if we realize that we must return to God the fruits of whatever talents He gave us, and if we believe that such talents are, in a sense, an extension of God's grace, it becomes evident that undue interference with the flowering of such talents can become a serious responsibility for anyone who, through invincible ignorance or inveterate prejudice, makes it difficult, if not impossible, for an artist to work in a normal and healthy manner. This thought must be left to the tender consciences of some members of our diocesan building commissions!

If we look at the history of architecture we find that each age has produced a distinct architecture, informed, it is true, by elements of design from various sources, but without any particular reference to style as we have come to accept that term today. Art and architecture were always modern in their times and they were modern in the best sense of the word since no one called them so. History also furnishes us with continued evidence that the great artists and architects of the past worked out their problems with imagination, daring, creativeness, a sense of proportion, and some intuition—all qualities we badly need today. Because of the greatly accelerated tempo of the times we are now faced with a challenge, which is to seek a revival of the best elements of past ages amidst the chaotic conditions of the present. And we must escape the tendency to fall into the extremes of unbridled self-expression.

We may be tempted to mourn the fact that we were not born in those "golden days" of church architecture— the thirteenth century, for example—when we could have been numbered among the myriad of "anonymous" artists who produced the cathedrals we all so admire and often understand so little. The fact is that we live in the here and now, that God's divine plan obviously makes it imperative that we immerse ourselves in the world as it is, that we develop to the fullest extent whatever capacities or talents God has given us and that we return to Him, through the ready and cheerful acceptance of our responsibilities as children of God, the fruits of those capacities and talents, informed by the graces that any well-balanced person has received from the Creator. To shun our times, to mourn for a vanished past, can only bring us to a spiritual vacuum.

We cannot, of course, talk in terms of centuries when we attempt to present the history of religious art in the United States. We have telescoped a great deal of change into a comparatively short time; a very short time if we think of the centuries which nurtured the Romanesque or Gothic periods, for instance. The early days of this country's existence and the pioneer expansion to the West are really, in the context of history, in the quite recent past. Think of Oklahoma, admitted to statehood in 1906, which has already produced works of significant religious architecture. Pioneer conditions seldom led to the creation of beauty. We began our national artistic life in the shadow and under the cloud of post-renaissance exaggerations, further aggravated by the execrable taste of the Victorian Age.

As a reaction to this spate of Victorian Gothic and other stylistic aberrations we witnessed the attempt, prior to the First World War, to turn back the architectural clock. It was an attempt fated to fail, since the proponents tried to instill life into the ashes of a dead past. It was a look backward, an attempt to interpret tradition in the light of a static archeologism rather than in the light of a dynamic and ever forward-looking inspiration.

After the Depression in this country, and more particularly in recent years, economic conditions, perhaps more than convictions in the matter, have dictated a radical change in architecture, whether of a religious or secular nature. It has become increasingly more difficult to design or build churches in a pastiche of a dead style. The structural and decorative forms which characterized those past styles were impossible to realize in the face of rising costs and budgetary stringency. Simplicity has become a necessity, and this simplicity has left the architect face to face with his talent, with mere book knowledge generally useless. And it is not easy to be simple, yet not sterile! These conditions, in turn, have led the talented architect to solve his problem in the light of the primacy of the liturgy: his plan must function. This change of direction has not always been an unmixed blessing. The archeological die-hards can now retreat behind poor copies of the new idiom in architectural design, for there are so many badly designed churches called "modern," to the delight, of course, of the vacuous critic!

In a recent book,[2] edited by that perceptive critic, Peter Hammond, one of the collaborators, Lance Wright, traces what he terms the three marks of modern architectural expression: "the sense of the provisional," "the sense of economy," and "the sense of the continuing nature of space." He points out that the sense of the provisional seems to arise because of the rapid rate of change in modern life. Earlier architects built as though for eternity; they were building monuments. Today the search for monumentality does not correspond to reality as we see it. Recent mastodontoid structures in a number of American dioceses contradict this characteristic in their curious search for expensive and mediocre monumentality. The second mark of modern architecture, that of economy, also contrasts sharply with the attitudes we have inherited from the Renaissance. The population explosion and the consequent spatial needs for each person have greatly increased. Although building methods have improved, increased costs of production and high labor wages make economy imperative and a well-managed budget is a necessity. It may not be amiss, here, to point to the paradox that the client who is hampered by a low budget better serves that budget by seeking the services of a practitioner of high repute or of a young architect of imagination and daring; in any case the client should shun the low-fee hack. The stiffness of the fee will be more than offset by the savings which the intelligent architect will effect for his client, for he will not waste money in meaningless decoration. To design with distinction, with simplicity, and within the limitations of a tight budget is not easy. It is then that the client should seek intelligence of a high order.

As for the third mark of modern architecture, the sense of the continuing nature of space, Mr. Wright compares such spatial continuity to a leaven. He points out that this contrasts with traditional instinct which is to enclose space whereas spatial reality calls for a change of outlook in the form of architectural openness which, in turn, will "leaven" the laity toward an apostolate which has always been theirs but which has been latent. Here again I would suggest that members of diocesan building commissions ponder these matters. For, it all holds together whether we think of our life in the here and now or whether we think of implementing those ideas on the practical level of building to enclose a congregation gathered for the celebration of the liturgy.

In all these matters of reform we are again brought back to the intangibles and the solutions depend on the talent and vision of the architect and, we can add, the humility of the client. It is only right that we seek those reforms that cut into established patterns of usage and remove the outcroppings of mere habit and misunderstanding. Many patterns of habit are too often an unjustified and spurious kind of conservatism. True conservatism, just as dynamic tradition, preserves the essentials but is willing to shear off any wild growth.

If we are to put first things first as regards the primacy of the liturgy we must also place first things first in regard to the practice of all the arts in the service of the Church. Etienne Gilson[3] has clearly enunciated this principle in this fashion:

If one wants to practice science for God's sake, the first condition is to practice it for its own sake, because that is the only way to learn it. . . . It is the same with an art; one must have it before one can put it to God's service. We are told that faith built the mediaeval cathedrals: no doubt, but faith could not have built anything had there been no architects and craftsmen. If it be true that the west front of Notre-Dame is a raising of the soul to God, that does not prevent its being a geometrical composition as well; to build a front that will be an act of charity, one must first understand geometry.

We Catholics, who acclaim the high worth of nature because it is God's work, should show our respect for it by taking as our first rule of action that *piety is never a substitute for technique;* for technique is that without which the most fervent piety is powerless to make use of nature for God's sake.

There is one difference that must be observed between present conditions in the United States and Europe which is a difference our foreign friends delight in exploiting. The long tradition of great art in European countries has produced, in time, a climate of art that is lacking here. I believe that is why instances of a revival of a vigorous and creative religious art have so frequently occurred in Europe these past decades, particularly in Germany and Switzerland. After all, the more one knows, understands, and is surrounded by, great art of the past, the more one is likely to be of the present, and so to be modern in one's art.

However, we, in the United States, are slowly reaching a measure of maturity. The major factor in progress will be the entrusting of the design and decoration of our churches to the most creative artists available, and, in many cases, to artists and architects who may not have yet worked for the Church. Today's need for simplicity also demands a new breed of professional man. What a challenge is offered to us! And where should such a challenge be met with vigor, with imagination, with enthusiasm, if not in a church? Just as in the normal evolution of the liturgy, the beauty of our religious architecture is born of the necessities of the times.

Once the architect of talent accepts the temporal discipline of his task, he is on the way to achieving that beauty we all seek in the House of God.

There has been a welcome change in this country these past ten years. Twenty-five years ago those who felt that religious art should share in, indeed should express, the changing times were on the defensive. They were accused of belittling the great achievements of the past; they were accused of scorning tradition; they were accused of attempting to foist on the Church the aberrations of "modernism." Today, however, the precursors who saw clearly the practical and artistic applications of the primacy of the liturgy, as it affected the normal and healthy evolution of art, are now in a position of dominance. It is the pseudo-traditionalists, the sentimental escapists, who must justify their views.

And when we are subject to the well-worn commonplace, "We must give the people what they want"—really the height of inverted snobbery since it too often means, "Yes, I know art and might appreciate its fine flowering today, but my people are too far behind"—we can read Sir Herbert Read's fine commentary on that attitude:

It is for society to catch up the artist—not vice versa. And such has always been the rule. The great artists of the past never put a brake on their development so that "the people" could catch up. Art is conditioned by the highest intellectual understanding of a period; or is inferior and decadent. Even when art was most socialized and "integrated," the actual business of patronage was still in the hands of an exclusive clique of connoisseurs—the highest ranks of the priesthood in the Middle Ages, for example. The people accepted the art that was imposed on them; we have absolutely no evidence that they understood or appreciated it— especially no evidence that they appreciated it for the aesthetic value which constitutes its title to be called art. Art is socially functional, but it has always functioned through the intellectual élite of any period. Any other view would compel us to reverse our values, to exalt peasant art above the art of the élite. Admittedly the élite themselves are a function of the sociological process of history. And admittedly *the proletariat of to-day is the élite of tomorrow.*[4]

So, to *play down to the people* is hardly paying them a compliment nor is it leading them to a higher level of appreciation and understanding of art.

We cannot now claim that we enjoy a generally favorable climate of art, at least on the official level, but we can claim that individuals have produced fine examples of religious art and architecture in many parts of this land. We can only hope that those whose arrested growth engulfs them in the vacuum of frustration and despair will get out of the way and allow others to work in peace and increased productivity.

Another encouraging sign of the times comes from the work of our young men in the universities, the rising generation. The imaginative approach of many of these young men should mean progress in the coming years, providing the roadblock of prejudice is removed or made less maddening through some degree of humility. The imaginative approach should also gradually lead to a realization of the need for the work of our finest and most talented painters, sculptors, stained glass artists, silversmiths, mosaicists, and all the craftsmen; in short all who can bring beauty back in our churches.

In this respect we have reached a point when we might well call for an ecumenical council of the arts; a meeting of minds which could help to integrate into the fabric of all the arts the hidden treasure of those artists whose present religious vacillation is not caused by lack of talent but rather by the absence of that discipline through which they could channel their efforts. But the discipline I refer to takes place within the broad and generous context of the Church qua Church and certainly has nothing to do with that intolerable discipline qua censorship of ignorance or prejudice of persons within the Church.

What art needs today, and particularly religious art, is the generous acceptance of its travail and a willing and vigorous sponsorship of artists of talent who yearn to work for the Church. It would be a great blessing if the Fathers of Vatican Council II should liberate the arts from the frustrations of recent centuries of unhealthy inbreeding and so allow the artist freely to return to God the flower and fruit of his talent!

NOTES

[1] *The Spirit of the Liturgy*, translated by Ada Lane (New York: Benziger, 1931), p. 125; italics added.

[2] *Towards a Church Architecture*, edited by Peter Hammond (London: Architectural Press, 1962), pp. 234–237.

[3] *Christianisme et Philosophie* (Paris, 1936); quoted from Yves Congar's *Lay People in the Church*, translated by Donald Attwater (Westminster: Newman, 1957), p. 372.

[4] *A Coat of Many Colours. Occasional Essays* (London: George Routledge & Sons, 1946), p. 246; italics added.

11

The Sacral in Liturgical Music

CLEMENT J. McNASPY, S.J.

Catholicism today, partly as a result of the renewed stress on the doctrine of the Mystical Body, tends to see herself in dynamic rather than static images. We hear more of the Church adapting and developing; less of her unchangeable structure. While, of course, there is a strong core of immutability, given by God, we have learned to view the Church in her historic and fluctuating condition, as she adjusts to her members' needs. The very summoning of Vatican Council II in terms of an *aggiornamento* shows the acceptability of some levels of change.

Recently, for example, Heribert Schauf expressed even so central a theological problem as the relationship of pope and bishops in terms that certain earlier theologians would hardly have found tolerable: "The Church is not like a circle, with a single center, but like an ellipse with two foci."[1] This ellipse image has also been used by other contemporary theologians (Karl Rahner, John Courtney Murray, among others), and *mutatis mutandis*, it seems a happy one to apply to other facets of Catholicism.

In a well-known passage, Newman speaks glowingly of "Catholic fullness," as opposed to an alleged primitive simplicity or "purity." Rather than "simplicity," we prefer to see Catholicism as a *complexio* or *reconciliatio oppositorum*. Some years ago, E. I. Watkin described *The Catholic Centre*, in a stimulating volume that has become classic. There we read that Catholicism occupies a "central position between all extremes and one-sided excesses, reconciling and balancing them, rejecting only their denials, their exclusions and their partialities."[2]

This reconciliation must not be reduced to Hegelian relativism, nor must it be thought of statically, as something done once for all. Tension, rather, or polarity, seems a more appropriate term with which to describe something as precarious and shifting as the type of balance that one should be prepared to find in the large areas of Catholicism that are human, as opposed to what God has revealed. Erich Przywara, years ago, in his *Analogia Entis*, prepared us for this type of thinking, as he discovered the presence of polarities in all created reality, even apart from divine revelation. It is no wonder, then, that we expect them at every level of our knowledge: the Creator/creaturely,[3] the transcendent/immanent, the eschatological/incarnational, and other abstract tensions; and the sacral/profane, universal/local, popular/professional, social/individual, progressive/conservative, structured/liberal, classic/romantic, and any number of other more concrete formulations.[4]

The liturgical/personal tension has been widely discussed among Catholic liturgists and other thinkers. Fr. Léonce de Grandmaison, many years ago, found it useful to insist again on the importance of personal prayer, in a masterly

little work of that name. More recently, Jacques and Raïssa
Maritain took it upon themselves to warn against what they
called "pseudo-liturgical exaggerations," by way of defense of
contemplation.[5] Two splendid articles by Josef Jungmann
and L. Malevez throw considerable light on the tensions to
be met most acutely in liturgy.[6]

It is the aim of this essay to focus on several of these
tensions inasmuch as they bear on liturgical music. All too
often, the writer has felt, liturgists have found it difficult to
hold a dialogue with musicians, not merely because of what
may be thought "vested interests," but, perhaps more, because of a problem of communication. Each group had no
trouble conversing with members of its own group, but
could make little headway with those of the other. This
paper, I submit, could be subtitled "Prolegomena for a
Dialogue."

Sacral/Profane

Ever since Rudolf Otto's *Das Heilige* became the stock-
in-trade of religious anthropologists and psychologists, the
word "sacral," like "numinous," "mythic," "archetypal,"
has become as modish as "existential" among philosophers.[7]
Prescinding from the abstract and rational aspect of religion (on which Catholicism has ever insisted, particularly
during the scholastic and Counterreformation periods),
Otto studied the terrible power found in one's encounter
with God.

It was, of course, the feeling of awe and terror before the
mysterium tremendum, as well as the *mysterium fascinans*,
an experience which he describes as "numinous," "wholly

other," totally different from the merely human.[8] Mircea Eliade has discussed and developed these concepts many times over, and even nonreligious students of religions like Emile Durkheim find it useful to stress them.[9]

All known religions insist on a division between what may be called the *profane* and the *sacred*. The *sacred* may be applied not only to spirits, but to rocks, trees, springs, places, rites, expressions, formulas. The essential thing is that it be *apart*, separate—"Odi profanum vulgus et arceo," sang Horace, not in a snobbish mood (as is often said), but echoing the authentic sense of the sacral.[10] The holy is what one does not touch, does not discuss, often (as in the case of the Divine Tetragrammaton YHWH) does not even pronounce. Respect, love, or terror define its exact boundaries,[11] and the stress on these several ingredients will vary from religion to religion, and from epoch to epoch. Much of the Old Testament, for example, stresses respect and even terror, though love is already the first commandment.[12] The New Testament, of course, goes much farther in the direction of love and intimacy—"God *is* love" and "The Kingdom of God is *within* you."

The Christian stress on the sacral has itself presented a tension. When Our Lord stressed the religion of "spirit and truth," He did so against a background of exaggerated, often soulless ritualism. Yet, we know that the apostles continued to attend the Temple after Christ's ascension, and that the development of a separate Christian liturgy did not take place in a day. Evidently, unless we are to assume that the apostles completely misunderstood their Lord, Christianity was not meant to be entirely "interior." Yet, there remains the interior pole or focus, and throughout Church history we find certain saints strongly emphasizing it, even to the apparent neglect of the exterior, when periods of worldliness seemed to call for a renewal in the other direction: St. Bernard, St. Francis, St. Ignatius Loyola, Charles de Foucauld, among others.

Today the problem seems especially acute. The humanism of our time, more than ever before, is founded on knowledge and technology. Publicity, rather than mystery,[13] seems to be our motto. As Pierre Colin put it, "The rule of the engineer has succeeded the rule of the sacred."[14] Physics scrutinizes atoms, biology tries to re-create life itself, psychology plumbs the depths of the soul, astrophysics and newer sciences plumb those of space. Everything is brought to light; everything is rational.[15] If ever there was need for liturgy, for ritual, for the sacred, that time is now; yet when could the problems surrounding ritual be so serious?[16]

The very tradition of all liturgy stresses the sacral. Urs von Balthasar enumerates the ways this is done: by a sense of religious "good taste," a sense of what is proper and fitting, in the attitude of man facing God.[17] For while the Roman liturgy (just to mention the one we are most familiar with) is not without its moments of boldness—for instance, "O felix culpa" and "mirabilius reformasti"—it keeps a balance of serenity and hierarchical order.[18] Yet, how does the man of today reach the sense of the sacred? Must he retire to a monastery, to a neo-gothic cathedral hidden among skyscrapers, to a bare chapel of Charles de Foucauld, or to the "neo-brutalism" chapel of Le Corbusier?

There lurks a snare, of course, in too casual an acceptance of the terms "sacral" or "holy." H. Richard Niebuhr has pointed out how easily the bogus in this area may be taken for the authentic. "The sense of the holy is diffuse," he writes; "in itself it is not polytheistic, henotheistic, or mono-theistic. But by means of social ritual, doctrine and tradition it is organized and directed toward certain objects or events."[19] Thus, one may make an idol of the impressive, as the sacred mountains or groves of the past. Indeed, one need only walk through the giant redwood forests of California, in their awesome silence, to feel how easily primitive man could have become deviated in his quest of the sacral. Modern man, obviously, is somewhat more sophisticated in his idolatry, since he "finds and experiences mysterious sublimity in the works of men—in great music, in the breathtaking spans of great bridges, in soaring towers." And even more subtle, and perhaps more insidious are the "numinous symbols of the social unity"—flags seen as sacred objects, military reviews exciting feelings of collective grandeur and glory, and even documents of national history treated as sacred books.

The apparent answer, as Niebuhr suggests, lies in "the sanctification of all things. Now every day is the day that the Lord has made; every nation is a holy people." This pseudo-sanctification can mean the total evaporation of the holy. For, if everything is treated as equally holy, then nothing is holy, nothing truly sacred.

Yet another element in the human response to the sacral lies in the "desire for ecstasy, for transport out of the ordinary round of routine . . . of increased sensitivity, of enlarged views."[20] Romano Guardini has related this to the play element in the liturgy,[21] "all on the supernatural plane, but at the same time corresponding to the inner needs of man's nature." Long before, Plato had noted the need for play. "Life must be lived as play," he stated in a famous passage.[22] Whether Guardini had Plato explicitly in mind, he goes on to show how the fact that the "life of the liturgy is higher than customary reality, it adopts suitable forms and methods . . . it speaks measuredly and melodiously; it employs formal, rhythmic gestures; it is clothed in colors and garments foreign to everyday life."[23]

The play element in liturgy has been developed by Johan Huizinga. He notes that all religions have a "striking similarity in their sacrificial rites," and concludes to "a very fundamental, aboriginal layer of the human mind."[24] This does not suggest, of course, that liturgy is frivolous, since "genuine play can also be profoundly serious." It is noteworthy, in fact, that the chapter in Guardini that follows the "Playfulness of the Liturgy" is called "The Seriousness of the Liturgy." Huizinga shows that the sacred festival is "celebrated" on a "holiday" or "holy day," and regardless of the seriousness, and at times the frightfulness, of ceremonies, "the whole thing has a festal nature. Ordinary life is at a standstill."[25] Independently, Karl Kerényi pointed out the same phases of contact between liturgy and play, stating that the two share a certain primacy and absolute independence[26]

The impact of this sacral/profane tension in the realm of liturgical art, and specifically of liturgical music, may now be examined.

Some years ago, following the restoration of St. Stephen's Cathedral, Vienna, Fr. Josef Jungmann ventured a few doubts regarding the new brightness and lightsomeness to be felt there. These are values, doubtless; but, he added, "it is another question whether its fourteenth-century architect would have been equally satisfied."[27] For, the old church, like many others from the Middle Ages and earlier, conveyed a sense of reverence and awe from the moment one entered.

One of the functions of art in the liturgy is precisely to heighten the sense of the sacred. A church is, in great part, a holy place. True, unlike the ancient temple, which was only the shrine of the deity, the Christian church has the further function of being a home for God's "holy People"— *plebs sancta*—where God's Word will be given, and where sacrifice will be offered.[28] In fact, for the Christian the most important element of a church is the fact that it is the place where the People of God assemble, the place for the community.[29]

The extraordinary mood created by certain churches in the Spanish tradition can hardly be forgotten by anyone who has visited them. Santiago de Compostela, for example, continually reminds one that it is a holy place, a shrine; and the combination of mysterious space and darkness in Toledo and Seville cathedrals, together with the elaborate grille screens, emphasize profoundly the solemnity of the holy sacrifice. The Moslems who built the great mosque of Cordoba, too, knew how to create a holy space, especially in the spot reserved for the holy book; and the appalling "cathedral" carved out within the mosque only accentuates the tastelessness of a later generation.

At the other pole, of course, are certain baroque and modern church structures, where all is light, clarity and gaiety. These, it need hardly be said, are authentic values; but, if the church is to fulfill its whole purpose, the values must not be allowed to obliterate or frustrate the sense of holiness. True, there was once the *disciplina arcani* (by which the holiest parts of the liturgy were kept away from the unbaptized), but today our taste and temperament run rather in favor of intelligibility.[30] However, liturgy must not sink to the level of mere rationality, or it will fail to symbolize the majesty and otherness of God. Plainly, this has repercussions in the realm of architecture, stained glass, and statuary.

In music, too, the implications are serious. Music's negative functions in the liturgy are principally a break from the prosaic, worldly, profane street outside, and a sort of refuge from the times.[31] Somewhat as architecture heightens and sanctifies space, music intensifies time and may easily be a symbol for sacred time.[32] This more *positive* role we meet again in the liturgy. In the psalmody of the Divine Office, for example, we are not in the presence of musical *expressiveness*. The same set of melodic formulas are used for words of very different meaning. But the elevation of the voice into simple recitative song—oratory at its highest—does solemnize and intensify the words. The Pater Noster, too, based on four notes, is not an exciting expression of each petition, much less of each word; rather, it is an emphasis which somehow accentuates the hieratic and sacral quality of the prayer, in a way that would be inconceivable without music. Paradoxically, the sort of music here used adds solemnity, but does so in an impersonal way, unlike an oratorical declamation.

Nowhere will the sacral/profane tension be more striking than in liturgical music. Perhaps it is the relative permanence of the visual arts—architecture, sculpture, mosaic, etc.—that helps to give them a continuity of "meaning."

Obviously, a Greek temple or a Gothic church do not "mean" the same to us as they meant to their creators. Symbolism and personal satisfaction of creation apart, they were felt with a different set of "overtones" by those who made them. Both styles seem to us ancient and even quaint, charming; to their creators and contemporaries they were *dernier cri*, though again *dernier cri* did not hold the same fascination to them as it does to our fashion-conscious tastes.[33]

But the very impermanence of music, its fragile quality, its need to be reactualized time and time again, its precarious dependence on a variety of performers—all leave room for an immense range of subjectivity. Leonard B. Meyer has demonstrated the dependence of music on "the cultural context . . . Apart from the social situation there can be neither meaning nor communication," he shows. And further, "an understanding of the cultural and stylistic presupposition of a piece of music is absolutely essential to the analysis of its meaning."[34]

Thus, what sounds like music to one culture or one epoch may sound like intolerable noise to another. Even a slight experience with oriental music will bear this out; however, within our own tradition it is always a source of amazement when one learns that thirds and sixths, which we consider the basis of "normal" harmony, were during much of the Middle Ages considered dissonant, while fifths and fourths, which traditional harmony rules out, were then considered "normal." Further, a few centuries before, no harmony existed at all, and that is the case in most cultures apart from our own.[35]

Accordingly, it requires considerable training in various

styles before one can appreciate them or understand them, and even more before they communicate as they were intended to communicate. It is evident to musicologists that the music of the sixteenth century did not exert the type of emotional tug that it does on us. Palestrina, for example, did not seem altogether "serene" and "otherworldly"; much less did he give the impression, as he did to a famous nineteenth-century composer, that in his music "nothing happened." On the other hand, some of the most ravishing and worldly of madrigals from the sixteenth century sound quite religious to people who do not understand the language today. An interesting test may be made by playing some of Luca Marenzio's love madrigals, or those of Claudio Monteverde, for listeners who do not know Italian. They will believe this worldly music to be quite "liturgical," "churchy" and "sacral."

An example close to hand is Hassler's famed lied *Mein Gmuet ist mir verwirret* ("My peace of mind is shattered"), which we know as "O Sacred Head Surrounded" from Bach's treatment in the *St. Matthew Passion*. Long association has made the song seem quite religious; yet originally it was a profane love song. This class of chorales was known as *contrafacta*, or parodies, and became a normal type of composition in the sixteenth and seventeenth centuries.[36]

An extreme case of subjective association in the distinction of sacral and profane occurs in the attitude of the early Church toward the music of Greece and Rome. The classic works here are the treatments of Gérold and Quasten,[37] in which hundreds of texts from the Fathers of the Church are cited. Certain instruments are expressly prohibited because of their association with pagan cults or worse.[38] St. Jerome advises a young Christian to be "deaf to the sounds of instruments."[39] Diodorus of Tarsus explains why instruments have been "abolished from church, in favor of the simple chant."[40]

Aristotle and Plato, and those Greeks within the Pythagorean tradition, were exceedingly insistent that certain types, and only certain types, of music should be used, especially in the training of the young.[41] The *Politics*, in fact, dedicates whole chapters to the role of music in education —not only to music in the broader sense common to Greek usage.[42] Cicero, following the Greeks, exerted a considerable influence on early patristic opinion, and we find him insisting on the moral benefits or harm of specific modes.[43] This was further developed by Cassiodorus, who, in line with Greek moralistic thinking, assigned specific moral and psychological qualities to the different modes.[44] The fact that the Gregorian modes have been found to be altogether different from the Greek modes bearing the same names shows how arbitrary and even fantastic much of this thinking was. It is an extreme case of "associationism," which we have discussed, and shows again how difficult it is to assign the concept "sacral" absolutely to music of a given type.[45]

Popular/Professional

Another perduring tension in liturgy and the liturgical arts derives from the twofold aim of both: the glory of God and the good of souls. Not, of course, that the two are altogether distinct, but they do represent, again, two foci. If the purpose of worship were simply praise, it could conceivably be a work that might best be delegated to "professionals."

The problem is exacerbated today by the heightened prestige of specialization in all realms of human endeavor, even the fine arts. Until about a century ago, on the other hand, a composer was presumed to be a performer; not so, today. And, until relatively recently, it was not exceptional for a painter to be a sculptor too, and possibly even an architect. Leonardo da Vinci and Michelangelo differed from other artists not so much in their versatility as in their quality of performance.

Today we are living not so much in a world of *The Two Cultures*[46] as of many cultures. Musicians, like other artists, are so intensely specialized that they find it hard to communicate with ordinary persons of their own time. Smaller and smaller areas of arts (to put it another way, many "isms") are cultivated by professionals, who find it increasingly impossible to meet the sensitivity of other than a small cabal or coterie. And this altogether apart from any latent snobbery or avant-gardism.

Some of the problem is, obviously, a consequence of cultural acceleration: we have no time to catch up with artists before they have moved to another discovery. Over a lifetime of composing, Palestrina did not move stylistically as far as Stravinsky sometimes does between single compositions. Thus, just when the ordinary listener has come to grasp, say, *The Firebird*, we find that the composer has advanced through at least five other styles, leaving even sensitive listeners some fifty years behind. The problem is disturbing enough in the concert hall; in church, however, it becomes distressing. For, although one may take a contemptuous attitude toward a mere audience—at the price of money, however—what does the liturgical artist do in the presence, not of a cultural proletariat, but of God's "holy People"?

Recent papal directives on sacred music have made an effort to recognize the presence of this polarity. With the insistence on popular participation, there has also gone a recognition of the value of "art" music, particularly the Roman school of sixteenth century polyphony.[47] This latter is surely music of high professionalism, requiring trained choirs, and in no sense adapted to popular participation. Yet, with the recent stress on participation, little wonder that church musicians have become alarmed and inclined to feel left out.[48] Fr. Jungmann has wisely called attention to the danger of complex music being excluded. "In the heat of battle," he says, "such things have been said. These must be seen in the context of the battle of a young struggling movement." He goes on to make an observation that is useful throughout this discussion: "As elsewhere, thesis and antithesis must be followed here by a synthesis which will unite in a higher unity what is valuable in both positions— not as in a sheer compromise, but truly in a higher unity."[49]

Liturgy is, of course, the public, social worship of God done by the Mystical Body, the Church. As "public, social worship" it is done by the Church as a whole, and this suggests the role of participation, congregational singing.[50] The people must not be nor be thought to be "detached and silent spectators"; worship must not be allowed to degenerate into a "spectator sport."[51] On the other hand, the Mystical Body is not a monolithic body—it is living and organic. This involves a variety of functions, hierarchical and popular. Just as certain prayers have traditionally been reserved to the celebrant, other functions to deacon, others to subdeacon, and others to acolytes, so it seems fitting that in the artistic part of cult there will be a distinction of roles.[52]

This has been exhaustively discussed by Fr. Joseph Gelineau in his recent study *Chant et Musique dans le Culte Chrétien*.[53] Not only in the Roman rite, but in all the rites of the Church, such a structuring of roles takes place, and in periods of the history of our rite which we are apt to consider "golden" (especially the time of St. Gregory, pope from 590–604) there was never a question of everybody singing everything. Even in monasteries which are dedicated to the liturgy in a special way, like that of Solesmes, there is a "division of labor." The gradual, tract and other elaborate chants are not sung by the entire choir (though surely it could be, after so many years of experience), but by a specialized group of cantors.

The problem of a musical vernacular, as well as a linguistic one, rises here.[54] Even if one is to be an intelligent listener, he needs some familiarity with a given style. Much of the repertory of Gregorian chant is not only hopelessly difficult for any but a specialized *schola*, it is almost meaningless even to any but trained listeners. After many years of personal dedication to the "cause" of Gregorian, not a few musicians have wondered whether the effort was not uneconomically invested. Even in those happy—but, oh, so rare —parishes where Gregorian is performed and heard in a reputable fashion, one wonders whether the superhuman travail required was not misplaced—or at least, whether equal results or superior ones might not have been achieved at less cost of time and absorption. The situation is, obviously, quite different in monasteries, where the chant may be thought of as a (monastic) vernacular, like Latin itself.

No trained musician would question the *artistic* quality of the Gregorian repertory as it has come down to us, least of all when one is privileged to hear it at Solesmes, Montserrat, Saint-Benoît-du-Lac, or other monasteries. Moreover, it does offer the great advantage of being a music altogether *apart*, with the suggestion of the "holy," the "sacral." As much as Romanesque and Gothic architecture, or Byzantine mosaics, the chant is associated (in our minds) with worship. But just as Gothic or Romanesque were not so *apart*, so *totally other*, in the day of their vital creation, but were rather part of a total cultural style (when warehouses, bridges, schools and dwellings were all just as Gothic or Romanesque as churches), so the chants may once have been less *other* than they seem now. This does not, of course, invalidate their usefulness in creating a mood of holiness in church today.

It does suggest, however, that we are only looking at one pole of the tension—the *otherness* pole. Granted that chant has this happy result, just as Gothic and Romanesque architecture do; does it follow that it is fully relevant to people living today? Sacred architecture must be sacred (and at least somewhat *other* than the profane), but if its *otherness* is identified with the past, with the dead-and-gone, is there no danger that the image created by it of religion will suggest something of the past, something dead-and-gone? And is not the danger of using too much music of the past—the palpably remote past—just as pertinent? Does it not suggest that religion is simply quaint, archaic, and irrelevant? It is quite understandable that those for whom Gregorian has become a business or "vested interest," or those whose psyches are altogether impregnated with it, so that it has

become a living language of musical experience, would tend
to give it an importance that it may not now deserve. Yet,
the fact that the Church has often presented it as offering a
model for liturgical music (which no one would dream of
questioning), and the fact that it will, within the foresee-
able future, remain a part of our musical tradition, and a
very large part, should not lead us to imagine that an exclusive diet of Gregorian is best for the spiritual vitality of the
normal twentieth-century Christian.

Another facet of this popular/professional tension is the
matter of estheticism, as though the liturgy were there for
the benefit of the connoisseur or creator. Guardini has some
harsh, but beneficial, cautions on the matter in his *Spirit of
the Liturgy:* "There is danger that estheticism may spread in
the liturgical sphere; that the liturgy will first be the subject
of general eulogy, then gradually its various treasures will be
estimated at their esthetic value![55] This should, obviously,
not lead to a puritanical revolt against beauty, but is a warning to put first things first. As Abbot Herwegen put it, "The
liturgy has *developed* into a work of art; it was not deliberately formed as such by the Church. The liturgy bore
within itself so much of the seed of beauty that it was of
itself bound to flower ultimately. But the internal principle
which controlled the form of that flowering was the essence
of Christianity."[56]

In the realm of liturgy, it would seem, beauty is something that emerges unself-consciously, somewhat like health
in a properly functioning organism. Sir Kenneth Clark's
observations about art and society seem equally relevant
here in our discussion of liturgical tensions: "A healthy and
vital relationship between art and society exists when the

majority feel that art is absolutely necessary to them, to confirm their beliefs, to inform them about matters of lasting importance, and to make the invisible visible. . . . When a society produces an art which is lacking in vitality and imaginative power, but which nevertheless seems to be accepted by the majority, there is something wrong with that society."[57]

Personal/Social

A number of other tensions may be noted in the liturgy, and, while it is not possible to treat them all in such a short essay, several of them do seem related to liturgy's double role: the individual and the corporate, the free and the hierarchical, liberty and formulation, the spontaneous and the stylized, the prophetic and the jurisdictional, adaptation and tradition, ex opere operantis and ex opere operato. Evidently, each of these polarities adds some nuance to its neighbors, and they are by no means synonymous—only analogous.

It is evident from the Gospels and the Acts of the Apostles that worship, like so much else in the nascent Church, was far less organized and ordered than it has become since then. Indeed, many of Our Lord's precepts seem to stress the personal and interior, rather than the corporate and exterior. "When you pray, go into your chamber and close your door," He instructed us. And again: "God is spirit, and His worshipers must worship in spirit and in truth." Yet we know that the Apostles and the apostolic Church early had a liturgy, and that, while relatively informal, it quickly took a distinct shape.[58]

The early Christians were prohibited by persecution and other restrictions from having vast places of worship, but tended rather to meet in houses, the term "house of the Church" being the oldest term for what we call "church."[59] No wonder, recognizing the fundamental difference between pre-Christian and Christian worship, Minucius Felix could even boast: "We have no shrines and altars";[60] for every Christian shared in the priesthood and was himself an altar. Not, of course, that every Christian consecrated. Informal as the early Church was, it was hierarchical in principle from the beginning.

We know little of liturgical music in the first few generations of the Church.[61] Recitatives akin to those we still use, or simpler melodic formulas like the Pater, Preface and other priestly chants, were very likely used almost from the beginning. We know that the great Eucharist Prayer (ancestor of what we call the Canon of the Mass) was at first improvised, and only gradually took on a set formulation.[62] There is a natural tendency of liturgical usage toward conservatism—a law of continuity. This is partly a psychological drive, and partly a symbolic recognition of the unchangeableness of God and the things of God amid human flux. Understandably, religious people are disinclined to tamper with what has been handed down.[63]

However, there is always the prophetic element in dynamic religion, and, within certain flexible limits, bursts of spontaneity have their place. Even today, a wide range of variety of homilies (really a part of the liturgy, and, ideally, not something whimsically tacked on) is permitted, and considerable latitude in the selection of music. Quite early we find St. Augustine holding forth at length on the Alleluia and *jubilus:* "The *jubilus* is a form of singing that means that the heart is bringing forth what it cannot put into words."[64] And again: "It means that one cannot express his joy and yet gives witness that what is conceived within cannot be explained in words."[65]

Any musician knows to what lengths this sort of spontaneity could lead, if allowed to singers untrained in tradition and taste. One shudders to think what could take place today, if there were not strict controls. Even sixty years after St. Pius X's *Motu proprio* one still has to endure the misguided spontaneity of singers and unskilled organists, as though personal piety and enthusiasm were a substitute for competence. St. Augustine's adage "Ama et fac quod vis" is hardly applicable here.

Yet, at the other pole, lies the problem of static custom, where music or other art remain in use after their meaningfulness has deteriorated. If the battle for contemporary architecture seems relatively won, that for contemporary music has hardly been started. Some of the problem may lie in contemporary music's remoteness from popular experience; architecture, generally, seems to be in a happier state at this point in our century, and this may account for the happier state of liturgical architecture too. One reason for this may be the fact that, while once a building is built, it is built; whereas, even after a musical composition is written, it is still at the mercy of performers. And a certain parsimoniousness in the matter of employing trained organists and singers leads few of them toward the service of God in Catholic churches.

The benefits of liturgical conservatism are, of course, obvious to anyone who reflects on the problem. In an age of cultural atomism, where change and fads are obsessive, and eccentric vagaries are treated as values, one needs the anchor of tradition—not only tradition in the technical and theological sense, but more broadly taken. Yet, the tendency to fossilization which Fr. Louis Bouyer deplores[66] has led to reactions that are quite the opposite of tradition. It is not unlikely that the growth of allegorism and proliferation of devotions during the later Middle Ages were owing to a want of adjustment to liturgical needs. Had Latin not become a "veil" rather than a vehicle of communication; had the faithful been instructed within the happy *discretio* (to use Dietrich von Hildebrand's phrase[67]) of liturgical balance; had they understood the centrality of the Church's official worship—would there have been that rush toward the peripheral and marginal in the matter of subjective, fringe devotions? It is at least thinkable that the Reformation need never have happened had the liturgy done its secondary function—the edification and help of the faithful—with anything like efficiency.

The healthy balance between social worship and private devotion is, owing to a long period of disengagement, anything but easy to achieve. And like everything else, it has strong repercussions in liturgical art and music.[68] The saccharine or pallid words in which even profound devotions have been costumed could only inspire music of the level of "On This Day," "To Jesus' Heart All Burning," "Good Night, Sweet Jesus" and other hymns that have not yet been exorcised from our churches.

On the other hand, an absorption with the merely "objective" carrying out of certain ritual observances helps lead to the excesses just mentioned. Too easily we use the phrase "Oh, but it's valid," referring to the *ex opere operato* efficacy of the sacraments. True, there is a way of celebrating

Mass that is certainly valid in a minimal sense, but the fullness of grace in what should be man's highest encounter with God on earth is surely far from reached. If the rites are carried out in a perfunctory, offhand fashion, one may expect the liturgical singing to be equally casual. Again, we still know churches where five or six Requiem Masses will be dashed through in three hours, with no apparent thought given to the "sacramental" value of the music. This point, regrettably, is too patent to need development.

Tentative Reconciliations

It need hardly be said that our work of resolution will never be done, given man's historical and transient status, and that one generation's reconciliation of opposing pulls may easily seem to another generation an irrelevancy. Granted the contingent and culturally conditioned needs of time or place, we can never be absolved of the obligation of finding our own way. To change the figure, we should be prepared to accept an impermanent vector, depending on the strength of the several tugging forces. Our generation, facing its need for a more socially oriented spirituality, has stressed the participational, communitarian, gregarious poles of worship. Another, perhaps, reacting against crude conformity and oversocialization, may find it necessary to refocus on the interior, the personalist, the I-Thou (as opposed to the We emphasis). The mystic, transrational, sacral stress may prove, at one time, to be more appropriate in one century than in another, when light, clarity, rationality seem more in order.

All of these ingredients will always be at work, and we

impoverish our religious attitudes if we jettison any of them in favor of its opposite. For if the Church is one and many, local and universal, divine and human, transcendent and immanent, eschatological and incarnational, it goes without saying that the forms of her worship will reflect this complexity, and so will her liturgical music.[69]

Notes

[1] Heribert Schauf, *De Corpore Christi Mystico* (Freiburg, 1959), p. 307, n. 2. Reference found in Joseph Ratzinger, "Primacy, Episcopate and Apostolic Succession," p. 45, in *The Episcopate and the Primacy* by Karl Rahner and Joseph Ratzinger (New York, 1962).

[2] E. I. Watkin, *The Catholic Centre* (London, 1943), pp. 1–2 and *passim*.

[3] See my article "The Christian and Created Things," in *The Current* (Harvard), for October, 1962.

[4] The special isue of *Social Order*, May–June, 1953, is unusually rich in insights to the tensions involved in Christian humanism. See especially, articles by H. A. Reinhold, John Courtney Murray, John LaFarge, and W. Norris Clarke. *Nouvelle Revue Théologique* has, over the years, published a number of magisterial articles touching on these problems: L. Malevez, "La Philosophie Chrétienne du Progrès" (April, 1937; pp. 377–386); Pierre Charles, "Créateur des Choses Visibles" (March, 1940; pp. 261–279); A. de Bovis, "Le Sens Catholique du Travail et de la Civilisation" (April, 1950; pp. 357–371); Emile Rideau, "Science, Philosophie et Religion" (May, 1950; pp. 449–467). And there are the classic works by Pierre Charmot, *L'Humanisme et l'Humain*; by Jaime Castiello, *A Humane Psychology of Education*; and Emile Masure, *Humanisme Chrétien*, among many others. The world wide enthusiasm for Teilhard de Chardin's work is surely related to his serious effort at solving the tensions in Christian humanism. See Henri de Lubac, S.J., *La Pensée Religieuse du P. Teilhard de Chardin* (Paris, 1962).

[5] Jacques and Raïssa Maritain, *Liturgy and Contemplation*; translated by Joseph W. Evans (New York, 1960), pp. 85 and 88 esp.

[6] In *Nouvelle Revue Théologique*: "Liturgie et Prière Privée," by

L. Malevez (November, 1961) and "Sens et Problèmes du Culte," by Josef A. Jungmann (October, 1960; pp. 823–839). Both articles offer helpful supplementary bibliographies on the subject.

[7] See Herbert Schade, "Sakrale Kunst" in Stimmen der Zeit (January, 1963), pp. 274–289. The article is a study of several important recent works on contemporary liturgical art, especially of Karl Ledergerber, Kunst und Religion in der Verwandlung; Anton Henze, Moderne Christliche Malerei; Herbert Muck, Sakralbau Heute; Hugo Schnell, Zur Situation der Christlichen Kunst; and Guenter Rombold, Die Zukunft der Sakralen Kunst. Otto's book was first published in 1917 and has appeared in several translations and editions since then.

[8] See Mircea Eliade, The Sacred and the Profane (New York, 1959), esp. pp. 8–18.

[9] Emile Durkheim, The Elementary Forms of the Religious Life (Glencoe, Ill., 1954), pp. 37–39.

[10] Odes iii:1:1. Less famous but similar formulas may be found all over classic literature. For example, "Procul, o, procul este, profani" (Aeneid vi:258); Ovid Fasti 6:440; etc.

[11] See Jean Onimus, "Le Monde Moderne et le Sacré" in Études (November, 1962), pp. 166–178; and R. Caillois's long study, L'Homme et le Sacré (Paris, 1950).

[12] Rabbi Abraham Joshua Heschel's masterly work, God in Search of Man (New York, 1959), even in its title suggests the Old Testament stress which has always been vital, especially in Orthodox and Conservative Judaism.

[13] The term "mystery" has several meanings which at times seem to be opposed. In speaking of "mysteriousness" in this essay, I do not intend to refer to "mystery" as sign or sacrament whereby the visible serves to signify and clarify the invisible, but rather to "mystery" under its aspect of hidden and awesome.

[14] Pierre Colin, "Le Sens Chrétien du Sacré" in Christus (October, 1960), pp. 458–472. This issue of Christus is, in fact, a symposium called "Le Respect du Dieu."

[15] Jean Onimus, op. cit., p. 178.

[16] Pierre Colin, op. cit., p. 472.

[17] Hans Urs von Balthasar, "Liturgie et Respect" in Christus (October, 1950), pp. 473–487, and his great work on Prayer (New York, 1961).

[18] Urs von Balthasar, *op. cit.*, p. 476.

[19] H. Richard Niebuhr, *Radical Monotheism and Western Culture* (New York, 1943), pp. 51–53.

[20] *Ibid.*, p. 55.

[21] Romano Guardini, *The Spirit of the Liturgy* (New York, 1935), in the chapter called "The Playfulness of the Liturgy" (in the original "The Liturgy As Play"—"Die Liturgie als Spiel"), p. 181.

[22] *Laws* 7:796.

[23] Guardini, *op. cit.*, p. 181.

[24] Johan Huizinga, *Homo Ludens: A Study of the Play-Element in Culture* (Boston, 1955), p. 20.

[25] *Ibid.*, p. 21.

[26] Karl Kerényi, *Vom Wesen des Festes* (quoted by Huizinga).

[27] Josef A. Jungmann, "The Sense for the Sacred," in *Worship* (May, 1956), pp. 355–360. This is one of the clearest enunciations of the sacral-profane tension to be found in English.

[28] See the two symposia on church architecture published in *The Furrow* (September and November, 1962); Fr. Placid Murray's leading article, "Liturgical Principles for Church Architecture," pp. 449–515, is especially helpful.

[29] The work of Peter Hammond has brought this out especially well: *Liturgy and Architecture* (New York, 1961).

[30] C. J. McNaspy, "A Plea for Intelligibility," in *Liturgical Arts* (November, 1954), pp. 2–3.

[31] C. J. McNaspy, "Popular and Professional," in *America* (March 16, 1963), p. 383.

[32] This is much developed in several works of Susanne K. Langer (*Philosophy in a New Key* [Cambridge, Mass., 1957], *Feeling and Form* [New York, 1953], and *Problems of Art* [New York, 1957]). Basil de Selincourt treats the theme in his "Music and Duration" (*Music and Letters*, Vol. 6, No. 3, pp. 286–293). For example, he says: "Music is one of the forms of duration; it suspends ordinary time, and offers itself as an ideal substitute and equivalent. . . . [as] an analogy or foretaste of the experience of eternity."

[33] Le Corbusier, *When the Cathedrals Were White*, and the various works of Emile Mâle, Von Simson, Panofsky. The great Gothic cathedrals were originally not gray, much less "ancient." And we know that Greek sculpture and architecture were so brilliantly

colored that we should find them garish. They were far from neo-classic.

[34] Leonard B. Meyer, *Emotion and Meaning in Music* (Chicago, 1956), p. ix. The whole volume is a major breakthrough on the psychology of music.

[35] This is a commonplace in music history. For a brief summary see Donald Jay Grout, *A History of Western Music* (New York, 1960), pp. 68–69; 105; 158.

[36] See Grout, *op. cit.*, pp. 231–232.

[37] Th. Gérold, *Les Pères de l'Eglise et la Musique* (Paris, 1931) and J. Quasten, *Musik und Gesang in der Kulten der Heidnischen Antike und Christlichen Frühzeit* (Münster, 1930). I am particularly grateful to the musicologist James McKinnon for many references, especially in the following eight notes.

[38] See Clement of Alexandria, *Pedagogue* 2:4, and Quasten, *op. cit.*, pp. 86–109.

[39] *Epist.* 107.

[40] *Quaestiones et Responsiones*, 118.

[41] Plato, *Republic* 3:395–403; Aristotle, *Politics* 8.

[42] *Politics* 8.

[43] *De Legibus* 2; *De Finibus* 1:21.

[44] *Varia* 2:50 (*Migne* 60).

[45] Gustave Reese, *Music in the Middle Ages* (New York, 1940), pp. 27–50, esp. p. 45.

[46] The text of Dr. F. R. Leavis' celebrated and explosive lecture, *Two Cultures? The Significance of C. P. Snow*, is now published in an American edition, by Michael Yudkin (New York, 1963). The intensity and abusiveness with which the controversy between Leavis and Snow, and their disciples, was carried on in 1962 suggests the timeliness of Leavis' question.

[47] Cf. *Motu proprio* on sacred music of St. Pius X (my translation and commentary, published by Gregorian Institute of America, 1947); Pius XII's encyclical *On Sacred Music*; and *Sacred Music and the Sacred Liturgy*, instruction of the Sacred Congregation of Rites, 1958.

[48] *America* (March 16, 1963), p. 383.

[49] Josef A. Jungmann, *Pastoral Liturgy* (New York, 1962), p. 353, and note, referring to Pius Parsch, *Volksliturgie. Ihr Sinn und Umfang* (Klosterneuburg, 1940), p. 331.

[50] This especially applies to the simpler texts and responses (Amen, Et cum spiritu tuo, Kyrie, Sanctus) which have a popular origin and may be expected to be less complex in their musical form. See Gelineau (cited below, n. 53) and Jolly (cited below, n. 69).

[51] For a related problem, see my article "Has Music Become a Spectator Sport?," in *Musart* (January, 1963), pp. 6–8.

[52] See encyclicals, *Mediator Dei* and *Mystici Corporis*, with pertinent texts from St. Paul.

[53] Joseph Gelineau, *Chant et Musique dans le Culte Chrétien*, (Paris, 1962) is perhaps the major work covering the whole field of music in worship. With enormous scholarship and the French gift for clarification, Fr. Gelineau focuses on most of the problems arising, and offers balanced solutions to them, where solutions are possible.

[54] See Angelus A. De Marco, *Rome and the Vernacular* (Westminster, Md., 1961); Paul Winninger, *Langues Vivantes et Liturgie* (Paris, 1961); and my articles, *The Vernacular Re-Viewed*, (published as a pamphlet by the Liturgical Press [1961]), and "Should Mass Be in English?," in *America* (December 16, 1961).

[55] Romano Guardini, *The Spirit of the Liturgy*, pp. 195–196.

[56] Ildefons Herwegen, *Das Kunstprinzip der Liturgie* (Paderborn, 1916), p. 18. There is a rich bibliography available on this tension.

[57] Sir Kenneth Clark, "Art and Society," in *Harpers* (August, 1961).

[58] Gregory Dix, *The Shape of the Liturgy* (Westminster, 1945), esp. pp. 141–155.

[59] See Josef Jungmann, *The Early Liturgy* (Notre Dame, Ind., 1959), *passim*, esp. pp. 10–39.

[60] *Octavius* 32:1.

[61] See Karl Gustav Fellerer, *The History of Catholic Church Music*, translated by Francis A. Brunner (Baltimore, 1961), pp. 9–32; and Alec Robertson, *Christian Music* (New York, 1961), pp. 18–31.

[62] Jungmann, *The Early Liturgy*, pp. 39–51.

[63] Jungmann, *Pastoral Liturgy*, pp. 91–92.

[64] *Enarr. in 32.2.* "Jubilus sonus quidam est significans cor parturire quod dicere non potest."

[65] *Ennar. in 94.* "Gaudium non posse explicare et tamen voce testari quod intus conceptum est et verbis explicari non potest."

[66] See Louis Bouyer, *Liturgical Piety* (Notre Dame, Ind., 1954), the whole of Chapter 18, but esp. pp. 244–246.

[67] Dietrich von Hildebrand, *Liturgy and Personality* (Baltimore, 1960), Chapter 8, "The Spirit of *Discretio* in the Liturgy."

[68] See Joseph Cunnane's article, "The Relationship Between the Liturgy and Devotions As Expressed in Church Interiors," in *The Furrow* (September, 1962), pp. 531–544.

[69] Since this essay was written, three important studies of the sense of the sacral have appeared, which I shall review elsewhere: Gerardus van der Leeuw, *Sacred and Profane Beauty: The Holy in Art* (New York, 1963); Louis Bouyer, *Rite and Man: Natural Sacredness and Christian Liturgy* (Notre Dame, Ind., 1963); Bede Griffiths, "The Sense of the Sacred," in *Good Work*, vol. 26, no. 2. Directly bearing on our subject is a very thoughtful article in *Études* for April, 1963, by Yves Jolly, "Vie Liturgique et Musique d'Église." This, too, I would have used in preparing this essay, had it appeared earlier. A synopsis of Fr. Jolly's article, made by myself, can be found in the June, 1963, issue of the *Catholic Mind*.

12

LITURGY AND ECUMENISM

ROBERT W. HOVDA

Both in the hearts of Christian people and on the levels of scholarship and action there is today a convergence of a number of movements in contemporary Catholic life. One thinks immediately of the liturgical revival, ecumenism, the rediscovery of the layman, secular autonomy, biblical criticism and proclamation, new directions in ecclesiology. The chapter titles of this volume are a catalog of such movements.

The fact that one cannot examine thought and activity in any one of these areas without repeatedly encountering the others is excellent evidence that they are both sound and deeply interrelated. In these few pages I hope to confine my remarks as much as possible to the effect of the Catholic liturgical revival on the newly-popular (in American circles) ecumenical movement.

Recognition of the close relationship between these two efforts is almost universal outside the Church and quite general within it. Informed Protestant and Orthodox believers inevitably list our liturgical movement among the top few "most-hopeful-for-ecumenism" developments in twentieth-century Catholicism. The distinguished Presbyterian theologian, Robert McAfee Brown, in his *Spirit of Protestantism*[1] proves that this appraisal is not unique to what we think of as the "liturgical" confessional groups.

A few years ago, it was precisely this estimate that added fuel to the burning resentment of Catholic antiliturgical reaction. If some Protestants claimed for their traditions the quite undeserved distinction of being inspiration, norm, and goal for Catholic reform in public worship, a number of Catholics were only too happy to concede and even enhance their claims. The orthodoxy of our liturgical pioneers had made these status-quoers uneasy. If this rapidly growing gadfly on the sacramental corpus could be identified with what the same minds still considered the arch-enemy, we might relax again with a feeling of well-being.

Events secular and sacred—most important among them, the Vatican's Secretariat for Promoting Christian Unity (which should give us critics of bureaucracy pause)—have focused all the formerly dispersed Catholic ecumenical efforts and given them an effectiveness, persuasiveness, and popularity that are incredible. But I don't think this could have happened had it not been for the last fifty years of liturgical scholarship and popularization.

Not because the attempts to revitalize public worship in the Catholic Church have been "protestantizing" in cause or effect. Quite the contrary. The elements of the Catholic liturgical tradition in the various Protestant confessions bear painful witness to the fact of their sixteenth-century origins. Liturgical movements in the Anglican, Lutheran, Presbyterian and Free Churches are concerned not only with a "return" to sacramental worship but also with the purification and reform of those late medieval practices and prejudices which influenced their ancestors no less than they influenced ours.

So, if the Catholic liturgical revival's relevance for the ecumenical movement is not a matter of swinging us to a uniquely Protestant way of thinking about worship nor a devaluation of the sacramental sphere to meet the demands of this or that iconoclasm, what are the real reasons for the congeniality and interdependence of the two? I shall be brief in discussing several of them:

The Liturgical Revival and the Image of the Church

We seem to agree that the question "What is the Church?" lies at the heart of all ecumenical endeavor. And we know that this question has been confused no end on all sides. In American Protestantism, for example, the "Social Gospel" ascendancy earlier this century didn't exactly clarify the Church's definition. Nor has American Catholicism's preoccupation with an educational system.

Once the liturgical revival had emancipated itself from its monastic nurture, it addressed itself immediately to that central question. Its present pastoral orientation contributes to ecumenism a definition of the Church uncluttered by secondary and peripheral considerations—the Church is a worshiping community. Whatever auxiliary services or other aspects the image of the Church conjures, it is its fundamental, essential, incarnate self in the eucharistic assembly of the community ("at Mass," in our modern Esperanto).

Anything else the Church is or does is appropriate insofar as it flows from and relates to community worship. To
hold this is not to divorce secular life from Christian influence. It is simply to affirm that the structures and institutions, the means and the aims, of the Church *as Church*
are not identical (and should not be) with those of the
Church considered as citizens of a political society or members of an economic community. Influence, yes; identity,
no.

Such a clarification of the Church's image is a *sine qua
non* of progress in ecumenism. Great Protestant thinkers
like Karl Barth and Paul Tillich have been quite as insistent
as modern Catholic theologians in their cry, "Let the
Church be the Church!" As long as we Catholics could
hide behind our proficiency in one or another nonessential
Church activity, we distorted this image and made dialogue
that much more difficult. The fact that we are beginning
to face squarely—thanks to the liturgical revival—our
rather poor performance in our essential task is all to the
good.

Wherever else we may have looked for these things in the
past, this revival is convincing us that there is no teaching
like the proclamation of the Word at Mass in readings and
in preaching, no broadening of Christian horizons like the
soul's unfolding in petition and memento "for all sorts and
conditions of men," no thanksgiving like the holy table's
sacrificial deed, no challenge to love like the sacred meal we
share, no mission like the one we receive from this con-
frontation with God and one another.

We can truly say, "Here is the Church." We can
abandon caricatures and half-truths and all retreats into the

realm of the abstract. And we can do this because tradition in the Church is a living thing, a well in which fresh water is continually springing up, and no blind following of inherited custom. Our customs have not produced the liturgical revival and this vision of the Church; they have been obstacles. A living tradition in which the Word of God and His Spirit are ever-active has produced it.

The Church we see here, in the eucharistic assembly, is a Church which our Orthodox and many of our Protestant brothers can understand. It doesn't solve the problems of faith and order which separate us, but it provides a firmament on which they can stand and be counted (and prayed about, and discussed).

The Liturgical Revival and the Gospel

If there are any Catholics who see the good news as a lengthy and miscellaneous collection of articles to be believed—and a host of catechisms proves there are—they are those as yet unaffected by a liturgical revival which has helped restore priority and proportion to the believer's affirmations. The more intelligible and meaningful our sacramental celebration of the mystery of redemption, the less prone we will be to allow any growth, however luxuriant, to obscure its Christ-centeredness and its simplicity.

Protestant fears of "Mariolatry," for example, and Catholic temptations to it, find their answer not in refinements of terminology (though these have their place in theology) but in the sober and embracing doctrinal content of the liturgy. Pious practices and "devotions" which seem "lunatic fringe" to all Protestants and to many

Catholics and Orthodox would not make spiritual eccentrics out of our people if a living liturgy played a significant role in their prayer-lives. But when the liturgy is for all practical purposes removed as an influence, as a psychological force, the field is abandoned to whatever is intelligible, whatever happens to touch living men and women.

The impact of the kind of organic comprehension of the Christian mystery, with which the Eucharist and the other rites of Catholic public worship if properly celebrated inform the faithful, has obvious relevance to the ecumenical movement. It enables dialogue, again because we are at home and completely comfortable on that common firmament accepted by the World Council of Churches in its profession of faith in Jesus Christ as God and Saviour. There are no strange islands of belief unrelated to this continent.

The Liturgical Revival and the Bible

At this writing, the first session of Vatican II seems to have delivered us from a Counter-Reformation stance which has made credible the notion that Protestantism is the religion of the Bible. The Council could do this, of course, because of the outstanding contributions of contemporary Catholic Scripture scholars and of theologians who have reexamined the relationship between the Bible and tradition.

Certainly the liturgical movement has played a significant role in laying the foundation for the Church's emphasizing again the unique normative value of the written Word of God. This is so not only because the entire Catholic liturgy is a mosaic of Bible readings, Bible songs and Bible texts. The roots of the primacy which our public worship so clearly gives to the "Book" go deeper than that.

They go back to the Old Testament examples of liturgical structure and to the primitive Christian fusion of Synaxis and Eucharist, of the Liturgy of the Word with the sacrificial meal—back to the primitive conviction that the sacraments, the signs of faith, are basically dependent on the Word to which faith gives assent. They involve a real distinction, defined in terms of inspiration, between the Church of the Apostles and the Church after the Apostles.

Ecumenical dialogue will still be faced with problems of interpretation. But the day seems to be at hand when it will no longer have to waste its strength in a kind of tug-of-war between Scripture and tradition.

The Liturgical Revival and the Sacramental Principle

I think that a kind of practical anti-sacramental attitude, thought by us to belong exclusively to Protestantism, has been prevalent among us for centuries. In Protestantism, it expressed itself by minimizing the sacraments, by reducing not only their number but also their importance in the Christian life. In Catholicism, it expressed itself (and continues to do so) by affirming their efficacy while attacking the signs themselves, by a "sacramentalism" more at home in mechanical engineering than in theology.

That this "get-done-with-it" approach, this impatience with and brutalization of the delicate world of sign and symbol, should appear as "magic" or as man's attainment of a "position of strength" in his relation to the Father, is only too comprehensible. The moment that sacramental efficacy becomes divorced in popular piety from the sacred signs-in-themselves, from signification, it becomes easy for the naturally commercial heart of man to think of sacraments in a horse-trader's terms.

The liturgical revival serves ecumenism as well as sacramental theology and a truly Catholic piety by re-evaluating the sign, the word, the gesture, the thing, and its relation to Christ and to the effect Christ intends. Things—all things—can speak to man of God. Every existent is worthy of reverence, attention, worship (recognition of value: "with my body I thee worship"). God uses this ability of words and things to speak to man. Salvation history is a history of sacraments, a sacramental history. Chosen things for the sake of chosen people, and both for the sake of all people and all things.

As the nascent reform of Catholic public worship establishes visibly and theologically the worth of things and the relationship between sign and effect, it will remove one of the dark clouds which now hang over the dialogue, obscuring it and tempting it to wander.

The Liturgical Revival and the Rediscovery of the Layman

It is doubtful whether any phenomenon of twentieth-century Catholicism has done as much to make us aware of the vocation and role of the laity as has the liturgical revival. I don't mean specifically the layman's role in the temporal sphere, although his autonomy and function in that area have been significantly clarified in modern Catholic thought, but rather his role within the Church and as the Church.

There is nothing perplexing about the fact that Catholic ecclesiology has been preoccupied ever since its emergence as a branch of theology with a defense of hierarchy and clergy. But its almost total neglect of the layman until recently has been more than perplexing—it has been disastrous. We have begun to repair the damage, although it looks from here like a long, slow process.

But even our beginnings are a great contribution to the ecumenical dialogue. Here our Protestant and Orthodox fellow Christians have much to teach us. The lay responsibility which they have structured into their executive and legislative agencies should become familiar to all of us as a guide and goal toward the Catholic recovery of a missing link (in what some have thought a rather adequate organization). They have done this, we should note, without rejecting (excepting Quakers, etc.) the ministerial function.

The priesthood of the faithful is Catholic doctrine, but it is Protestant practice. Our capacity to learn from their experience will partially determine the speed of our own renewal and will offer additional proof, if any is needed, that dialogue is a two-way street. They are delighted, as we should be, to hear contemporary Catholic theologians reassessing, for example, the traditional comparison between the lay vocation and the vocation to a life under vows.[2]

Ecumenism, then, is served by a liturgical revival which has established firmly the layman's normal and active role in the celebration of the Church's liturgy. That his responsibility in worship implies a responsibility in secondary and auxiliary aspects of the life of the Church is a conclusion missed only by those of us still suffering from nineteenth-century American or sixteenth-century European traumas.

Incidentally, as the theology of the laity matures it is bound to cast a light that may seem merciless on other roles in the Church—namely, those of bishop, priest, and deacon. It may seem that just as these bootless fellows have got out of the "sacristy," we are ready to push them back in. No doubt we can arrive at a satisfactory adjustment, but only if the clergy are willing to reexamine their vocation in the light of Scripture and the liturgy of ordination.

The Liturgical Revival and Variety in "Discipline"

The Catholic Church has always been in theory and in fact the home of many "sacred" languages, many kinds of ritual, many types of clerical and religious dress or undress, many ways of expressing essentially common doctrine, and so on. But we have somehow conspired to hide this variety from "Gentile" eyes, rightly or wrongly believing that it would compromise our witness to unity.

So, while variety has been preserved at least in one corner of the Church or another, the general impression we have conveyed is that of a conformity which neglects hardly a detail of the Christitan life. Now we find that the skeleton in the closet is the most important member of the family. The liturgical revival has not only drawn the veil from such variety as does exist but has impressed upon every Catholic interested in a vital public worship the necessity of a much greater variety and adaptability in everything from the catechumenate to burial customs.

This means, I think, that many common questions in ecumenical conversation can be open questions in the present state of affairs and we can concentrate on fundamental issues. Thanks to the liturgical revival, we are becoming aware that another Western rite (or several rites), besides the Roman one, is not beyond the realm of possibility and certainly not inimical to Catholic unity.

The Liturgical Revival and Legalism

When Luther looked at much of the Church in his day, he felt as Jesus did when He was confronted with the elaborate and scrupulous legalism of some of His Jewish brothers. Rules for everything, but no spirit; prescriptions which would bind in almost any eventuality, but no life. One does not have to read far in contemporary Protestant thinkers to note, despite their courtesy, a troubling suspicion that Catholicism is, in this sense, pharisaical.

We deserve this highly unpleasant image only if we forget the priorities and emphases I have already discussed as among the gifts, graces, of the liturgical revival. The dominance of the juridical element in our Western Catholic thought becomes considerably less overpowering when we begin to see the Church as a worshiping community.

Given the human animal and any body politic, rules are inescapable. But to keep them in their place, to refuse to give them "airs," to be free enough to change the rules for the sake of men and the Gospel—this is a difficult challenge. And it is a dangerous one for the Christian who is not yielding himself to constant formation in the school of liturgy.

Worship magazine has in its pioneering and wonderfully fruitful history neglected none of these areas of ecumenical concern. Its volumes offer a documentation not only of these few points I have made but also of other ways in which studies and pastoral efforts directed toward a dynamic, intelligible Catholic public worship have created a climate conducive to ecumenism. Its editor, Fr. Godfrey Diekmann, has been as intelligent and eloquent a champion of dialogue with Protestant and Orthodox Christians (before it was popular) as of liturgical vitality and renewal.

Depth and joy in commitment—and this, after all, is the aim of the liturgical revival—is anything but a handicap in ecumenism. Without it, there is no real "you" or "I" to speak, to share, to learn and teach. It is no advantage to the dialogue to keep Him who is love equidistant from all parties.

NOTES

[1] New York: Oxford, 1961.
[2] See John D. Gerken, Toward a Theology of the Layman (New York: Herder and Herder, 1963).

13

THE FUTURE: ITS HOPE AND DIFFICULTIES

FREDERICK R. McMANUS

In the fall of 1960 an entire issue of the magazine *Worship* was devoted to the liturgy and the spiritual life. In their contributions to the magazine, Cyprian Vagaggini and Bernard Häring had no difficulty in correcting the obsolete concepts of the liturgy which not long before had led the Maritains to propose a seeming opposition between liturgy and contemplation. What appeared to be a moment of crisis for the liturgical renewal, at least in the United States, turned out to be only the revival of an old quarrel on faulty premises.

Nevertheless, a related problem retains its vigor: the apparent abyss between public worship and personal holiness, or, to suggest at once how illusory the abyss is, between public piety and private piety.

Without minimizing at all the other obstacles to liturgical understanding, we must first recognize the challenge of those who divorce growth in the spirit from the sacramental life, especially since the challenge comes from respected sources. The indifference, hesitation, or antagonism of clerics when faced with the liturgy's progress, the deep-seated fear of change almost for the sake of the fear, the overwhelming task of liturgical education in the midst of a general crisis of religious education, the illusion (or pretext) that liturgical participation can be postponed until liturgical reform is achieved—all these are serious problems, so often enough considered that they need not be rehearsed here. They may indeed be more serious, but they are not found so deep as the dissociation of liturgy and piety.

As suggested already, on the plane of theory or doctrine, the quarrel is unreal. No one is so devoted to the scholastic scheme of virtues as to deny a place to faith and hope and charity in the liturgical exercise of the virtue of religion. There is little resemblance between a romanticized cult of silence (the so-called silent Mass) and true contemplation. It may be hoped that no one actually believes liturgy to be merely external worship; and if this is so, the quarrel is semantical.

At any rate, the promoters of the liturgical revival have been talking about interior worship all along, about spiritual worship, worship in spirit and in truth which is—as it were, secondarily—given an external and ritual expression.

The theory has not yet reached the givers of retreats, the preachers of missions, the spiritual directors, the masters of novices, the writers on spiritual formation. Progress toward perfection is still sought in an atmosphere of spiritual isola-tionism, except for the necessary contact with the ex opere operato essentials of the seven sacraments—with even these deeds of Christ and the Church conceived as individual-istically as may be.

A caricature of such an extreme position is not really un-fair. Fear of externals and fear of the community are indeed carried to extremes, as if we were created without tongues and voices to sing God's praise or as if we were redeemed without an Incarnation. Logically, the masters of this kind of spiritual life should prefer spiritual communion to sacramental communion, worship in the woods or fields to worship in church where one would be distracted by the presence of God's people. They should regret that the Divine Word took human flesh and blood and that they must look forward to a bodily resurrection.

It would be easy to undercut such a position, however logically it may flow from the fears of those untouched by the liturgical renewal. It is more profitable, however, to explain positively that the Christian liturgy is worship in spirit and in truth and that the prayer of God's people is no less personal and individual for being common and public.

The liturgy is the carrying on of the work of redemption, the function of the priestly office of Jesus. It is act of God and act of man: God's goodness and holiness descending, man's praise and prayer ascending. It is the expression—by Christ and by His members together—of Christian love of God and of the brethren.

In these terms there is no least cause for worry over externalism, formalism, or a "less than spiritual" worship. The words of the liturgy have inner meaning, they guide and direct, inspire and stimulate interior devotion. Far from being a concession to our human condition, the audible and visible sides of Christian worship recognize the wholeness of the human person as created by God—with lips to sing and legs to walk in God's honor.

If there is formalism in the often repeated phrases or gestures of worship, or if these lose their meaning in the course of time, it is the task of liturgical reform to correct the evil. But, even in the liturgical rites most in need of radical change, the smallest measure of outward participation represents some inner activity.

Thus to rise for the hearing of the Gospel—and, in better instructed communities, to rise after the consecration of Mass for the solemn offering of the Eucharist—reflects some religious meaning. When the people come together as an assembly, as the Church, their physical presence one to the other is a sign, a sacred symbol, expressive of an unseen reality. And well might the sound of psalm and sacred song, of dialogue and acclamation, the very noise of public worship distract the individual from his self-centered piety to the holy celebration of the mystery of Christ!

Already we are in the midst of the second error in which the liturgy of the Church is falsely placed at odds with personal piety. It is difficult to deny that worship of God should involve the body as well as the soul, and difficult not to see how song and spoken word may channel and stir up inner prayerfulness. But there is always the challenge of the community to the individual, always the fear of neglecting those things that are summed up in the catchword: "I have a soul to save"—by myself.

Small wonder that the bishops assembled for the Second Vatican Council determined that the liturgical rites should stress even more the communal nature of Christian worship. So long the emphasis has been in the opposite direction—in manuals of piety, in spiritual conferences, in books of meditation—that strong measures are needed to restore the balance. It is God's will that we, individuals that we are, should be saved as a Church, as a people, as His people.

The truth of the matter, however, may be said more

pointedly. Community worship is most personal and most individual. It requires, as an absolute condition for its worth, the deepest and strongest faith and holiness of each participant. It intensifies and enhances the personal piety of each participant.

Because an action—in this case, the action of worship of God—is done by and in a community—in this case, the Church—it is no less the action of each individual member of the community. In the Christian liturgy the prayerfulness and spiritual progress of each one is the greater because of the communion with the other brethren and with Christ the Head. What each one offers to the glory of God's name profits all unto salvation, as the Roman missal prays.

The community of the faithful is not the enemy of the individual but his strength. The liturgy does not suppress the piety of the participant but lifts it up, gives its growth and meaning in the assembly—because of the union with Christ and with His members.

It is curious that liturgy and spirituality can still be divorced in the minds of some, especially clergy and religious, after the encyclical letter of Pope Pius XII on Christian worship. Much of the burden of the pope's doctrine was the essential harmony and necessary interaction of public worship and private devotion. It is a lesson still to be learned.

A species of this problem is raised whenever the liturgy is confronted and contrasted with devotional exercises, of greater or less popular acceptance.

Fortunately the weaker of these practices fall of their own weight. The evening devotion of poor construction and slight doctrine is not really saved from extinction, when the numbers of participants dwindle, by tacking it on to the

Sunday Mass—to everyone's confusion. In the United States the Lenten devotions have not been put in peril by evening Masses on Lenten weekdays; the devotions were in general decline already, perhaps because they lacked Christian substance. No one can really regret that the Three Hours' Agony of Good Friday—with the fearsome sermons and third-rate music, but with little relevance to the mystery of Christ—seems to be yielding in favor of the Word of God, the prayer of the faithful, the veneration of the cross, the Holy Communion, which comprise the day's liturgy.

For the most part, promoters of the liturgical renewal have not pressed the issue or recited the woeful state of the public devotions, novenas, tridua, and the like. It is easy—and not unjust—to attack many such devotional exercises boldly: they are hardly Christ-centered; even the eucharistic holy hour is often diverted from the worship of the Holy Sacrament to some cause like promoting vocations. The Word of God proclaimed, the joy of Christians in the risen Lord, the very praise of God are all foreign to a large proportion of devotions. Rather, they still lean to marvels, favors, grasping petitions, and maudlin hymns.

Such an indictment is possible. Wisely, it has not been the path chosen by the liturgical movement. Feelings have been spared, and the poorer and meaner sides of devotional life have been left to perish of themselves. At the same time one may regret the false image of Catholic piety and doubt its actual popularity—except among its promoters.

The problem is present even in the lawful and laudable devotion to the Holy Eucharist. It would be a considerable exaggeration to suggest that St. Pius X rang the death knell of eucharistic devotions when he restored frequent Communion to the faithful. On the other hand, we can hardly expect any flourishing, spontaneous development of such devotions, at least to the extent that they serve or have served as a substitute for sacramental Communion.

Even to hint at the diminution of expositions, hours of adoration, benedictions, eucharistic processions, is to invite the charge of a "practical denial of the Real Presence" from those who put "Eucharist offered, Eucharist received, Eucharist adored" on the same level of divine plan and institution. The likelihood remains that, with the devotion of the people now directed to the eucharistic meal (and not to obediently "hearing Mass"), the accidentals in the eucharistic cult outside Mass will not flourish so widely.

In this delicate area, strangely enough it is the liturgical promoters who have fostered and strengthened a sound worship of the Eucharist outside Mass, more perhaps when all is said and done than those who have had doubts about the liturgical renewal. One example of this is the new life given to the Forty Hours' Prayer by the use of the vernacular litany, chants, and hymns—brought about by the efforts of individual pastors with liturgical awareness and, more especially, by diocesan liturgical commissions. It may be that the language of the people used in this annual eucharistic observance will save the devotion from oblivion.

Another, broader instance where the liturgical renewal has done more for a sound eucharistic cult than any multiplication of expositions is the holy hour with the pattern of a bible devotion or, alternatively, a bible devotion which on occasion is completed by benediction with the Blessed Sacrament. Perhaps here we have a solution to the seeming conflicts if the biblical-liturgical spirit can be infused into the exercises of eucharistic cult, otherwise weak and growing weaker.

In fact, the mere mention of the bible devotion—"the sacred celebration of the Word of God" is the language of the Second Vatican Council—points to the happy resolution of the divorce between liturgy and devotions, if not of the divorce some would maintain exists between liturgy and spiritual progress.

The bible devotion or vigil is liturgical in its pattern, structure, and prayer forms. It is scriptural in its entire orientation, consisting of the Word of God, proclaimed and unfolded, with the people's response—often in biblical psalms and canticles. The development of bible devotions as a kind of "liturgy of second order" should be sufficient evidence that liturgical renewal means spiritual vitality in the Church.

Even so, this unexceptionable practice has its critics. They were unmoved when the Bishop of Rome propagated the practice in his own diocese. Perhaps they are now unmoved when the entire Catholic episcopate assembled in council (with only 38 negative notes) has approved and urged the bible devotions.

This kind of criticism and reluctance, found almost exclusively among the clergy and religious, is nearly inexplicable. Just as difficult to explain is the continuing hesitance to admit the action of God and the Church in the sacred liturgy into the world of the spiritual life.

No easy answer is at hand to this worn-out obstacle faced by the liturgical apostolate: the illusory opposition between public worship and personal piety. The difficult answer, and the only sure one, was given by the Fathers of the Second Vatican Council: a program, at every level and by every means, of clerical and religious education in pastoral liturgy.

It is tragic that developments of the past few decades—

biblical, catechetical, theological, liturgical, pastoral—should have passed by the majority of those who must preach and teach and lead. The great hope is the determination of the bishops in council that the liturgical education of the clergy and religious should now be pursued.

Who could enumerate the tasks and the problems of the liturgical renewal, itself only one phase of the general *aggiornamento* of holy Church? The obstacles range from simple intransigence to the extraordinary fear, among some clerics, of almost any lay activity, liturgical or apostolic.

One problem not often discussed is the danger of compromise. Of course, to be sound and fruitful, both liturgical education/promotion and liturgical reform must be gradual, prudent, and careful. But the twentieth-century liturgical movement is too old and too wise to indulge in half-measures or compromise proposals.

A few years ago, at the beginning of a Liturgical Week, an American bishop urged the virtue of patience upon the advocates of the liturgical renewal. At the end of the same Week, he urged courage.

An uncompromising courage, not to say persistence and vigilance, seems to be needed. This is true on the level of parish congregational participation, on the level of the student and publicist, on the level of official liturgical restoration.

Without digressing too far or generalizing too much, we should recognize that the progressive, the advocate of change and renewal, is at a disadvantage. The extreme conservative or traditionalist has few problems; he need not develop his position or even his arguments, it is enough for him to oppose, to stand against all change or development.

He may know very well that his cause will lose or be diminished, but he still serves that cause best by remaining inert, inactive, and, although the term is pejorative, intransigent.

Not so with the advocate of change, in some circumstances called the liberal. He is more likely to think out his position, weigh every argument, and propose what seems both good and attainable. His praiseworthy devotion to truth and freedom, to a reasonable and equitable solution, may betray him. Having considered and embodied the legitimate claims of the traditional, having scrupulously avoided any apparent excess or extreme, he finds himself unable to bargain without grave compromise and genuine loss.

A concrete example, the object of much controversy, is the vernacular question. Pro-vernacularists, if they may be called such, have generally been moderate and most considerate of the hesitations of the arch-traditionalists. They have not unduly pursued the logic of their position by saying that every syllable of public prayer should be in the language of the ones praying or that, whatever else might be sought, the more significant parts of the liturgy and surely the essential signs of the seven sacraments should be in the language of the worshipers.

On the contrary, the pro-vernacularists have made minimal proposals and accepted the practical usefulness of gradual, partial concessions, according to the nature of the rites and parts of rites. The danger is that, having made every reasonable allowance in advance for the fears of those who simply oppose change, they should find even the most moderate program diluted and weakened.

This illustrates a danger in partial solutions and in compromise. Possibly the moral is that the progressive must take more advanced positions from the beginning to make his point more forcefully and to leave room for concession or bargain.

How much is lost to the Church when each step forward requires infinite patience and overwhelming proof. In 1962 an American layman, Philip Scharper, gave a major address on "New Horizons in Catholic Thought." He summed up persuasively and eloquently the current developments in all the Church's forward-looking movements. One observer reacted in this way: how bright the Church's future if these could be the starting points of Catholic thought for all the Church's members and especially for the leaders, lay and clerical. Instead, each point must be proved at length and bitterly, each development must face resistance and reaction.

The same case could be made for the doctrine of some papal encyclicals: If *Pacem in terris* of Pope John XXIII could be accepted as a starting point for further development, as a plateau already reached—instead of needing to win a gradual and reluctant acceptance; if, in the field of sacred liturgy, the teaching of Pius XII in *Mediator Dei* did not have to make its way ever so slowly, even now after sixteen years; if the progress already made in sacramental theology could here and now become the commonplace of the manuals and open the door to wider speculation . . . These may be vain speculations but they attest the need for persistence and courage as the Church looks to the future.

At a symposium on the sacrament of orders held in 1955, Bernard Botte drew several conclusions from a study of rituals of antiquity. Among these "fundamental convictions about orders" which the "Church recognized as her own from the earliest times" was the following: "Bishops, priests and deacons form the hierarchical structure of the Church, the body of Christ; and this hierarchy is willed by God—its members are chosen by him . . . Episcopal consecration is not a purely personal act by which one individual communicates the powers he possesses to another individual. It is the collective act of the episcopal body incorporating the newly elect into the ordo episcoporum. . . . The priest is no more an isolated individual than the bishop: he is incorporated into the presbyterium which assists the bishop in his ministry. The deacon, for his part, is subject to the bishop. The bishop with his priests and his deacons constitutes the supporting framework of the local church, just as the order of bishops constitutes the framework of the universal Church . . ."

Needless to say, the ordinary manuals of theology contain hardly a trace of this doctrine of the collegiate character of orders, elsewhere developed by the same author from patristic sources. Nor is it to be found in common clerical and lay understanding of episcopate, priesthood, and diaconate. The point here, however, is this: What a tragic loss that this profound doctrine, now recovered, should have to fight its way to acceptance! As with progressive papal doctrine or the current intellectual and apostolic developments in the Church, how much easier would be the course and how much more vital would be the faith if these could be the readily accepted starting points for further achievements.

Realistically, such battles need to be fought—and the enemy of the progress of Catholic thought, including liturgical thought (and action), is needless compromise and hesitance.

There are practical instances of this. In the parish or diocese, the precise degree of vocal participation by the people

—song, response, common recitation—may be only a superficial test of sacramental depth; but it is a recognizable test. The danger of half measures in such programs should be obvious. Endless delays are interposed before the participation goes from potency to act; the thing is treated as a novelty to be introduced apologetically and grudgingly; no one is tried beyond his endurance or extended beyond his perhaps apathetic capacity; the "dialogue Mass" is confined to this hour of Sunday morning or to that occasion; every concession is made to every difficulty; the discouragments of failure are turned into welcome pretexts for abandoning the endeavor.

Naturally, this picture is harsh and exaggerated, but the ways in which programs of liturgical action are compromised and frustrated could be multiplied indefinitely. The example is appropriate, too, because it permits a distinction between the necessary gradualness and the unwarranted compromise. No parish (or diocese) goes overnight from liturgical inertia to a pinnacle of enthusiastic external participation; each step must be taken with care and instruction —but the goal must be pursued with uncompromising vigor.

In addition, the goal must be pursued without fear. In this connection, the nature of the Church and the nature of the Church's worship are sufficient assurance that the goals are sound. In another connection also, there should be no fear, namely, when there is question of the weakness of existing forms and rites to fulfill the purposes of Christian liturgy.

Here a grave obligation is placed upon the scholar and the publicist. If he honestly points out the defects of the past and the present, the advocate of change is in an un-

welcome position. In the Church especially there is an unconscious attitude that attaches the immutability of God to
the human institutions of ecclesiastical discipline and worship. And there is a less than candid refusal to confess error,
even though the confession would itself be a help to vital
growth.

The promoter of the liturgical apostolate, then, must on
occasion speak with some risk although he neither intends
nor offers any irreverence to sacred authority. The liturgical
year is a jumble including unknown saints with little significance or cult in the Church universal; no harm is done
to faith or piety by admitting this. That the celebrant of
sung Mass should recite the texts which others are singing
is nothing else than an error, a historical blunder; we are
better off if this is recognized.

Sometimes the half measure or the compromise is an
official thing and there are notable examples in the past
decade of liturgical reform. In spite of principles that are
beyond question, the editors and compilers of the emended
service books or rubrics often held back—especially in the
1955 simplification and the 1960 code of rubrics.

Strong criticism of these liturgical reforms would be unjust because much has been accomplished and because the
effort thus far is provisional and even experimental. Yet
there are feasts still partially observed (as commemorations) which should have been suppressed; there was the
desired restoration of the frequent Saturday observance in
honor of the Blessed Virgin Mary achieved in 1955 but cut
back by technicalities in 1960; there was the meager revision
of the rite of celebrating Mass (1961), which did no more
than expose the need for a profound reappraisal. A curious

compromise was revealed in the new editions of the Roman missal: the occasional rites before and after Mass (Asperges, absolution of the dead) could be altered even textually, but the ordinary of the Mass was untouched, although its emendation is vastly more necessary and significant.

These hesitations and partial accomplishments have their own explanation. They are mentioned only as a reminder that half measures are not enough in the forthcoming revision of all the Roman liturgical service books.

This is not a plea for radical liturgical reform, nor does it profess to discuss specific changes in the words and forms of worship. Yet the vigorous clamor for change—now formally determined by the bishops of the Second Vatican Council—must at times be uncompromising, as examples will show.

The preparatory prayers of Mass confuse the structure of the entrance rite and are of disproportionate length. The offertory prayers, also too long, anticipate the eucharistic prayer and, for all their intrinsic excellence, obscure the sacrificial offering in the Canon itself; a couple of the prayers do not really belong in the Roman rite at all.

At first glance one would think that the problems of these two sets of prayers could be simply solved. Let them be located at low Mass as at sung Mass, that is, entirely subordinate to the introit and offertory psalms respectively. The faithful need never advert to them.

Not long ago the editor of a popular publication attempted this solution. In a text for congregational use he substituted psalm verses for the preparatory and offertory prayers. He acted in accordance with the traditions of the Roman rite, the true significance of these parts of Mass, and recent recommendations of the Apostolic See. Yet the cry of literal-minded pastors and faithful made the publication unsalable.

Emendations should be made, of course, in order that the sacred services may be the better worship of God. Sometimes a change may be a matter of indifference in itself and yet required by the mentality of the clergy or the faithful. There is no basic objection to the recitation of the four proper chants of Mass by the celebrating priest. Yet his recitation of these choral parts has almost turned them into presidential or priestly parts and now the question is properly raised whether the celebrant should be allowed to recite these chants even at low Mass.

The examples could be multiplied easily. There seems to be little desire for a thoroughgoing revision of the Roman Canon, provided minor errors are corrected, Amens are omitted, etc. Even here, however, perhaps one or other additional version of the eucharistic prayer is needed, like the alternative Oriental anaphoras, if only to give some relaxation to the rigidity of the Roman rite. And perhaps this more radical proposal must be closely examined if the lesser reform is to be achieved.

All this is intended to illustrate at every level of liturgical development that reasonableness of program or reform should not degenerate into false compromise. If too little is sought or attempted, doors now open may be shut. The vernacular issue again provides a final example. The Council of Trent decided against the vernacular because of the circumstances of a given period of a given century, but the door remained closed for nearly four hundred years.

Now, perhaps at some risk, well worth taking, the liturgical renewal should be pursued without fear or hesitation —in study, in action, in reform.

If the major portion of this essay summing up *The Revival of the Liturgy* has been spent on two obstacles in the path of revival, this has not been done in any spirit of pessimism. The danger of compromise and the continuing divorce between liturgy and the "spiritual life" are indeed problems, among other problems, but the horizon of the revival was never brighter.

These studies are written to honor Godfrey Diekmann as he completes twenty-five years as editor of *Worship*. The concept of the magazine and its first years belonged to Virgil Michel, but its present tremendous significance belongs entirely to Father Godfrey. It is a temptation to indulge in superlatives, but the excellence of *Worship* requires no elaborate praise.

For the record it should be stated that Father Godfrey is a sacramental theologian of distinction and influence, that he has spent himself generously and fruitfully as writer and lecturer and preacher, that he is a great and good priest held in the warmest esteem and affection. In the context of this volume, he represents the very best in the liturgical renewal of our times.

Another temptation is to assess the revival in terms of contrast with the days when Godfrey Diekmann assumed editorship of what was then called *Orate Fratres*. The contrast would be sharp indeed. It is perhaps better simply to suggest how, with all the obstacles and with all the tasks ahead, the liturgical revival has the brightest of futures in the providence of God.

The reason for this optimism is, simply and obviously, the will and spirit of the Second Vatican Council. The Council does not replace the efforts of individual popes and bishops, clergy and laity, much less the labors of dedicated promoters of the liturgical apostolate over many years. The Council is the sacrament, the great sign of the Church, it reflects the whole Church in the midst of which the bishops speak.

But the Council at a certain moment of history has crystallized the progress of decades and brought it all into focus. And this because, in its first period, the Council determined, irrevocably we may say, upon a course of renewal —in the first place, an *aggiornamento* of sacred worship.

Although the definitive work of the Council in the field of liturgy is not, at this writing, completed, the principles were agreed upon on December 7, 1962, with near unanimity. The meaning of this agreement of the episcopal college, to support and accelerate the liturgical renewal and to decree the liturgical reform, can hardly be overemphasized.

In a sense, the Council could only define the tasks: ritual emendation and accommodation, by the postconciliar commission; subsequent adaptation and development, by the territorial bodies of bishops; clerical and religious training, including that most important instruction of those already in the pastoral ministry; liturgical education and participation, by bishops and priests, teachers and leaders. In defining the tasks, the bishops gave the revival its greatest motive and impetus, for the conciliar document on the liturgy is a disciplinary constitution.

The immediate and practical significance of the Council's decision on the liturgy can best be seen in the series of norms given for the revision of the sacred rites. They are directives addressed to a postconciliar commission; more important, they manifest the Church's thinking on the liturgy.

First, the reformed liturgy is to take greater account of the hierarchical and community nature of Christian worship, with a clearer definition and distinction of roles and with new emphasis on the parts, especially the vocal parts, pertaining to the people.

Second, the reform is to be based on the didactic and pastoral character of the liturgy. Thus it is to be simpler, clearer, more comprehensible. The place for the proclamation of God's Word is to be greater, but the didactic function of all the parts and prayers is to be acknowledged, together with the need for the language of the people in larger measure.

Third, the reformed liturgy of the Roman rite must be susceptible of adaptation and accommodation according to the diverse traditions and cultures of nations and peoples. Thus the rigidity of the rite is once for all abandoned.

Already these and other matters of Chapter I of the conciliar constitution have been studied and commented upon, in the light of a summary published immediately after the first period of the Council. When the text itself is promulgated, a new stage of the liturgical renewal will open up—with promise of substantial reform in a period of a few years.

Over and above this direct meaning of the Council's action, there are certain other points to be made, in order to substantiate the hopefulness of today's liturgical outlook.

To begin with, the Fathers of the Council adopted a moving and eloquent statement of the liturgy's meaning in the life of the Church—as continuation of the priesthood of Jesus, as sign and sacrament, as the summit of the Church's action.

The remarkable and promising thing is the manner of expression, evident even in the published summary of the document. Biblical and patristic, it is a return to apostolic preaching, as one commentator put it. Reflecting the catechetical movement of this century and learning from it, the bishops gave an example of the proclamation of God's teaching with scrupulous avoidance of the excessively scholastic or systematic. This, it may be hoped, is the first step toward the restoration of a sound liturgical catechesis.

Next, the document—like the Second Vatican Council as a whole—has an ecumenical purpose, to do whatever will help to foster the unity of all who believe in Christ.

The outward aspects and overtones of the liturgical renewal are surely sympathetic to Christian unity. In the forthcoming reform the chief expectations lie in the greater emphasis on the Word of God in the liturgical celebration, in the use of the language of the people which will at least make the rites comprehensible, in the simplicity and clarity of structure and text—not excluding the suppression of "ancient pomp and medieval pageantry."

Such developments and accommodations serve the worshiping Catholic and the separated brethren as well. But the real meaning of the Council's concern for the liturgy in relation to Christian unity is this: the liturgy, especially the Eucharist, is the meeting place of conciliation and charity. As the Fathers of the Council bring their respective churches and the Church universal into a deeper penetration of the mystery of the Eucharist, we are inescapably closer to all Christians who seek to be united at the table of the Lord.

A last reflection upon the Council as a cause for strong hope in the liturgical revival has reference to the bishops themselves who have succeeded to the places of the Apostles.

Priests and laymen have done and will continue to do their tasks in the liturgical apostolate, as in every apostolic movement of this century. But the bishops are the prophets and the shepherds in the Church. They are the first witnesses to the faith, they guide and feed and govern.

This is by way of saying that the overwhelming agreement of the bishops concerning the sacred liturgy is the surest and soundest guarantee for the future. In a way unexpected, their practical unanimity attests to the genuine *sensus ecclesiae*, the will of the Church.

Such agreement was unexpected. In the English-speaking world, for example, some few bishops had fostered the liturgical movement zealously and enthusiastically, others had supported it actively but largely out of obedience to papal declarations; some had issued helpful directives to their priests and people, others had left progress to pastoral initiative. Very many had remained silent, presumably seeing the renewal as something strange and unaccountable, as it surely appeared to the majority of the clergy.

At the beginning of the Council, again so far as the English-speaking world is concerned, the profound commitment of the bishops to this cause was not known or appreciated. By the end of the Council's first series of meetings, the minority of bishops who still retained misgivings was small indeed. Beyond all question, the Church had accepted and blessed this movement, in which Pius XII had seen the workings of the Spirit of God.

It should not be necessary to explain at length how this

episcopal support for the liturgical renewal is a cause for optimism. There is no question of papal authority when the Bishop of Rome speaks and rules as it were alone, any more than there has been any question of the commitment of recent popes to the liturgical movement. But the papal authority is an abstraction far removed from the day-to-day celebration of the liturgy.

This has been evident in other papal teaching and legislation, notably in the field of social thought. It is something else again when the pope and the bishops speak together with a single voice—and so we may describe the conciliar action on the liturgy.

The bishops assembled in council under the presidency of the chief bishop exercise their care and charge over the whole Church. When they disperse to their respective churches they inevitably are invested with a greater unity of action and of purpose. The prospects emanating from the Second Vatican Council, in its first undertaking, are that the bishops will cultivate the liturgical renewal with the vigor of their common commitment in the Council itself.

No one can predict either the time needed for the first stages of ritual reform or the future progress of liturgical participation by all the people of God. The obstacles remain, the effort to be made may be no less exhausting than before, but the Council has already put a new and pleasing face on the liturgical revival—perhaps most of all because of this last factor, the assent of the bishops of Holy Church, which is the blessed assurance that this is, in the fullest sense, an Apostolic Work.